THE

POWER
POINT

THE
POWER
POINT

MICHAEL E. GERBER

HarperBusiness
A Division of HarperCollins*Publishers*

Grateful acknowledgment to Vít Hǒrejš for "How Pig and Bear Went into Business." The story originally appeared in *Twelve Iron Sandals and Other Czechoslovak Tales* by Vít Hǒrejš. Copyright © 1985 by Vít Hǒrejš.

"Song of Central Equilibrium" from *Tai-chi Touchstones/Yang Family Secret Transmissions*. Copyright © 1983 by Sweet Ch'i Press, New York. Reprinted with permission.

Excerpts from "The Red Wheelbarrow" and "The Hunter" by William Carlos Williams from *The Collected Poems of William Carlos Williams, 1909-1939, Vol. I.* Copyright © 1938 by New Directions Publishing Corporation. Reprinted by permission of New Directions Publishing Corporation.

The Power Point by Michael E. Gerber is available on tape from Harper Audio, a Division of HarperCollins Publishers.

Library of Congress Cataloging-in-Publication Data

Gerber, Michael E.
    The power point / Michael E. Gerber.
      p.   cm.
    ISBN 0-88730-466-4 : $15.95
    1. Success in business.   I. Title.
    HF5386.G278   1991   91-7730
    658—dc20   CIP

Printed in the United States of America

Designed by Abigail Sturges

91 92 93 94 CC/HC 9 8 7 6 5 4 3 2 1

To my mother,
Helen Gerber Aaron,
with all my heart

CONTENTS

ACKNOWLEDGMENTS

To everyone at The Michael Thomas Corporation who has gone the distance with me, especially John Fandel, Bill Creveling, Marijo Franklin, Lynn Davison, Guy Bogenreif, Janice Drescher, Swati Sengupta, Glen Christensen, Muni Cruz, Marsh Agobert, and our irreplaceable accountant and advisor, Dale Irwin; you have my unbounded love and appreciation.

To my children, Shana, Kim, Hillary, and Sam, who have never said "Why are you *doing* this dad?" I love you with all my heart.

To my assistant, Lindy Crawford, who made certain I wrote every day; where would I be without you?

To my editor, Virginia Smith, who nurtured me when I needed it the most; you were exactly what I needed.

To my publisher, Mark Greenberg, who trusted me from the beginning to the end; thank you.

And finally, and forever, to Ilene Gerber, my wife, my true partner, and my true love. Thank you for being there with me through all the worst moments as well as the wonderful ones.

HOW PIG AND BEAR WENT INTO BUSINESS

Pig and Bear decided to go into business.

"We'll make lots of money!" they thought.

Pig baked a bushel of potatoes and Bear fried a heap of doughnuts.

They went to the marketplace early in the morning to get the best spots. Nobody was around yet. The morning was clear and chilly. Bear had a nickel in his coat. After a while he went over to Pig's stand to warm up a little.

"How much for a potato?" he growled.

"A nickel for you."

Bear was about to say that he'd just wanted to ask, but then he changed his mind. He fished for the nickel in his fur, took the biggest steaming potato in his paws and crossed the road back to his stand.

The business is moving, rejoiced Pig. But since there were no more customers for awhile, and he hadn't eaten since they started at dawn, he crossed over to Bear's stand and bought himself a black raspberry doughnut for a nickel.

Bear was happy to have his first customer. He felt he should eat something before they started to flock. He went over to buy another baked potato. The move brought him luck. He had hardly finished eating when Pig was over for another doughnut.

Then business slacked off again until Bear bought a potato. Soon Pig was over again and Bear went right back to his stand with him to spend the earned nickel. Pig returned for a doughnut and soon they were going back and forth until they sold everything.

They counted the money, but:

"How strange, I have only a nickel," Bear said.

"And I have nothing at all," said Pig.

They couldn't believe it.

"We have sold all our merchandise," they kept saying, "but we have no money!"

But in vain they counted and recounted: they had only a nickel between them after the whole day of busy trading.

Adapted from
Twelve Iron Sandals by
Vít Hǒrejš

1.
THE POWER POINT AND THE POSITION OF ONE: A BUSINESS EXISTS ONLY AS IT IS PERCEIVED BY OTHERS

*In too many situations
we automatically
experience people
as "them"—not "us."*

*These jungle-type
habits of mind
are dangerous
to our species.*

—Ken Keyes, Jr.

This book is meant to be a prescription for building a successful business in a Free Market System.

As you will find out, it probably serves as well—if not better—as a polemic against such prescriptions.

Please excuse the apparent contradiction. I know that if you're patient, somewhere in the middle resides a truth worth digging for.

But, to get there, you're going to have to do some of the work.

You're going to have to stretch where I stretch, and let go where I let go.

In other words, you're going to have to be willing to play an always frustrating, but sometimes enlightening, game. A game I'd call:

"How do you provide an answer to a question that you know has no answer?"

In a Free Market System, that's the game called Business.

❊   ❊   ❊   ❊

To anyone with even a passing interest in the comings and goings of our Free Market System, of business in the United States, it should be apparent that the life of a business here is a precarious thing.

If the business is a good idea—that is, does all the right things in the right way and at the right time, and is lucky—it succeeds.

If it's a bad idea it doesn't.

Unfortunately, the truth is that for the people who invest in other people's businesses, for those who start a business of their own, or for those who work for either of the other two, most businesses turn out to be bad ideas; most businesses fail.

More frustrating is that in a Free Market System even the good ideas—the businesses that succeed—turn into bad ideas in time.

The weather changes. A new guy moves in across the street. People stop having babies. Somebody comes up with a better idea. Or—and this happens—someone comes up with a worse idea, but *implements* it better.

In short, a Free Market System provides one with significantly more opportunity to fail than it does to succeed.

What worked yesterday will most likely not work today, and that something works today is insufficient justification for planning to do it the same way tomorrow.

How to minimize the risk?

If eight out of ten companies funded by professional venture capitalists go under, how can anyone expect to do better? Shouldn't we be able to expect better in a world with so much information at hand, with so much technical and technological know-how at our disposal, and with so many trained managers?

For years, clients have been asking me those very questions.

Is there a more dependable way to identify a potential business winner?

Is there a common denominator one can use to take a more accurate measure of a business idea?

Is there a pattern—a template—one can use to evaluate a business and its likelihood of achieving significant success?

Is there something all great businesses do that can be replicated by other businesses wishing to become great?

Is there a way to clone greatness?

I believe the answer to each of these questions is yes.

This book is my answer to those thousands of clients and businesspeople who have asked me these questions over the years, as well as to the millions of entrepreneurs, would-be entrepreneurs, and managers I have never met to whom these questions are just as important.

In this book I have organized the fundamental principles which I believe form the foundation of every lasting great business into a template or model of greatness, the presence of which in any business would indicate with a great degree of certainty what I call the *success-proneness* of that business, and the absence of which would indicate that a business is not likely to pass the test of time.

The value of this template, a component of which I call The Power Point Matrix, is that it is timeless.

It transcends epochs, technology, industry, markets, economies, and geography.

It could have been used as effectively in the nineteenth century as hopefully it will be in the twenty-first.

It could be put to good work just as effectively in the emerging Eastern European Free Market experiment, as it could in our Free Market's attempt to recapture its own lost glory.

It could just as well be applied to a corner grocery store as to a semiconductor plant.

The reason it is so timeless, so transferable, is because it is founded upon the one sacrosanct requirement upon which the existence of every business in a Free Market System always has depended, and always will depend.

That is, to succeed, every business in a Free Market System must learn how to satisfy, better than its competitors, the *essential needs, unconscious expectations,* and *perceived preferences* of the four most important groups of people in its universe: the people who work for it, the people who buy from it, the people who sell to it, and the people who lend to it; its employees, customers, suppliers, and lenders.

It is the combined judgment of all of these people, these four Primary Influencers, upon which the ultimate success or failure—yes, the life or death—of every business enterprise ultimately depends.

Which brings us to our first rule of thumb.

And that is, in a Free Market System . . .

Businesses Only Exist Because People Want Them To

I hope that statement doesn't come as a big surprise to you.

It surprises me that most businesses seem to operate as though exactly the opposite were true.

As though people exist *because* of businesses.

As though God created businesses first, and only when the businesses were seen not to work did He create people to go to work in them, to buy from them, to sell to them, and to lend to them.

I know that's a dumb thing to say—I know it.

But it's an even dumber thing to *do*. Yet for many businesses it's standard operating procedure.

Which brings us to our second rule of thumb.

And that is, in a Free Market System . . .

People Are Regarded as a Problem to Most Businesses

Yes, to most businesses in a Free Market System people are regarded as a problem.

Not only the people who work in the business, but the people who sell to the business, and the people who buy from the business, and the people who lend to the business. All people are regarded as a problem. And they're a problem because they're so *unmanageable*.

When people are manageable they're not a problem any more.

They're invisible.

And that's what most businesses I have seen would like people to be. Invisible. Not a problem. Not needing attention. Pliable. *Easy.*

That's why there are systems in the world other than the Free Market System.

Other systems were created to eliminate the problem of people.

In other systems, people aren't a problem because it doesn't matter what they want.

Unfortunately, in a Free Market System you can't get away with that mindset for very long, and that's what drives everybody nuts trying to run a business in a Free Market System.

In a Free Market System one has to come to grips with the fact that there are all these people—needing, needing, needing.

Unfortunately, in a Free Market System, all of them are needing the same damn thing—MORE!

More of what?

More of Everything!

But don't people know that there's only so much a business can give?

Why aren't they understanding like us?

Like who?

Like businesspeople.

Like the guys who run the business.

Like the guys here in the business at the top.

Like the guys who own the business.

Like the guys who manage the business.

Like the guys who would like people to be more reasonable.

Like the guys like us, who want . . . what?

Who want MORE.

Who want more of what?

Of everything!

But a business can only give so much!

Who said?

❋   ❋   ❋   ❋

And that's the special relationship between businesses and people in a Free Market System.

In a Free Market System, businesses are invented by people for a very special reason.

But despite what most of us believe, businesses are not invented only by those people who go into business—the so-called entrepreneurs among us.

In a Free Market System businesses are invented by all of us—by each and every one of us.

The reason we invent businesses in a Free Market System, like ours in the United States, is to do one thing—and only one thing—to create MORE.

Businesses in a Free Market System are the instruments through which people get MORE.

In all other systems, businesses are the instrument through which most people hopefully get *enough* (but rarely do), while some people—some very few people—get the MORE that everyone else isn't getting.

But, in the Free Market System, *everyone* is supposed to get MORE.

The problem with the Free Market System is that when everyone doesn't get the MORE that they want, then "shit happens" (as a policeman friend of mine put it).

And, that's the part of the Free Market System called *Business,* which very few people in business seem to fully understand.

A business in the Free Market System is only justifiable in the minds of people—is only tolerated in the minds of people, *is only permitted to exist in the minds of people*—if the business learns how to give them MORE.

A business is intended to be a perpetual motion machine, the only purpose of which is to find ways to give people MORE!

A business is a mechanism designed to produce MORE for the continually rising expectations of people in a Free Market System.

And, in a Free Market System, the minute a business forgets these things, the minute a business stops providing MORE, the minute a business begins to ignore its sole purpose for being in a Free Market System—its *raison d'etre*—it ceases playing the game called *Business.*

It begins to play the game called *Goodbye.*

Which brings us to our third rule of thumb.

And that is, in a Free Market System . . .

"Service" Is an Incomplete Word

If everyone understood that in a Free Market System such as we have in the United States, the game called *Business* is all about creating MORE for everyone, we would immediately understand why "service" is an incomplete word: it doesn't include enough.

It doesn't include the employees. It doesn't include the suppliers. It doesn't include the lenders. It only includes the customers.

Service is an incomplete word because it says, "The customer is king!"

But as it works out in real life, the customer *isn't* king except in the mind of the customer.

To the employees the customer isn't king, he's often a pain in the ass.

To the suppliers the customer isn't king, she's often a problem waiting to happen.

To the lenders the customer isn't king, he's often a drunk hanging on to a wagon careening into a wall.

No, the customer isn't king to them—*they* are!

"If the customer is king," they all ask privately, deep in the hidden, deprived recesses of their longing hearts, "What about *me?*"

That's what everybody else is asking too: "What about me?"

That's what happens when we don't understand the game of *Business* as it's meant to be played in a Free Market System.

People start asking the most obvious questions.

It should be obvious that, by itself, a strong focus on the customer is insufficient to create a successful business.

There can be no such thing as effective customer service in a company where the employees are disenchanted, where the owners aren't making a decent profit, where the suppliers aren't getting paid on time.

In short, a strong focus on customer service is not only insufficient to produce lasting results in a company, but, in itself, makes lasting results impossible to achieve.

Which brings us to our fourth rule of thumb.

And that is, in a Free Market System . . .

There Aren't Any Good Answers for Long!

If, as we've already agreed, the purpose of a business is to serve as an instrument through which people in a Free Market System get what they want—and what they always want is MORE—then it is safe to assume that any business which comes up with MORE is serving its purpose well, and therefore survives. Any business which fails to come up with MORE is not serving its purpose at all, and therefore dies.

Which leads us to the unavoidable conclusion that every time a business comes up with an answer, that answer bears within it the seeds of its own demise.

Every answer in a successful business is only a temporary solution reached on the never-ending path toward the search for MORE!

Which means that for businesses operating in the Land of MORE, there aren't any answers, only questions.

And the questions all lead in the same direction—the direction that every sensible, aware, responsive, dynamic chief executive officer knows as the only way to MORE.

The way every successful business operating in a Free Market System for time immemorial, has followed. In search of the ineffable, the undefinable, the unknowable, the indisputably, irrefutably, pragmatically, unavoidably aggravating Holy Grail of MORE.

The only justification necessary being: "If *we* don't, they will. And if they find it first, our ass is grass."

Which leads us to our fifth rule of thumb.

And that is, in a Free Market System . . .

You Are Either the Lawnmower or the Lawn!

Which is where we began this little moralistic tale—that in a Free Market System, business is a precarious thing; your very *survival* is at stake.

And, in the Land of MORE, as we've already learned, if you don't survive it's because you didn't *deserve* to.

You weren't paying attention.

Somebody opened the gate and rolled in the John Deere while you weren't looking.

Suddenly your role was defined for you: your ass was grass.

The same way the role is defined for most businesses, every single day of the year, because they aren't playing the game called *Business;* they're playing the game called *Goodbye.*

What's sad is that they refuse to accept that there's a difference between the two games.

Yes, it's sad and it's true that most businesses, large and small, are living by rules of thumb that aren't rules at all, but the cover of the box they've laid down in.

They have stopped asking questions, and have come up with an unsuitable (that is, self-serving) answer.

❋   ❋   ❋   ❋

A close friend of mine is writing a book about the meaning of money. He says that few of us really understand what money is, we simply use it. He feels strongly that we're paying a big price for our ignorance.

I feel the same way about business.

Like money, business touches each and every one of us at every turn—our food, our clothes, our entertainment, our recreation, our health, our very life. Every choice we make is impacted by business in some form, creating some service or product upon which we depend, or have grown to depend, if not for our very survival, at least for the survival of the life-style we have grown to enjoy.

Every day, all around us, businesses are being born, living, struggling, and dying. Each of them, like each of us, is a unique being with a unique identity and a unique place in the world. All of the characteristics found in each of us—active or passive, creative or dull, passionate or stingy, growing or withdrawn—can be found in a business.

Yet, just as with money, few of us understand what this thing called business really is. We go to work in them, buy from them, and have opinions about them. But we don't understand them.

To most people, business is what goes on around us while we get on with our lives, something being done "out there"—at most a commercial enterprise, a place to make money, a place to go to work, a place to buy things, or a place that makes things we buy.

Few people seem to understand that business is much more than these individual factors.

In a Free Market System, business isn't what goes on around us while we get on with our lives, business *is* our lives!

Business is what we do, all we do, who we *are*.

In a Free Market System, business is the organized expression of our growing self-interest manifesting itself the best way it knows how.

Business is a living thing.

Look at our businesses and you'll know who we are.

❋ ❋ ❋ ❋

In a Free Market System everyone is touched by the allure of business, you can't get away from it.

Writers talk about the business of writing books.

Artists talk about the business of creating art.

Intellectuals talk about the business of communicating ideas.

Spiritualists talk about the business of raising our spiritual awareness.

Meditators talk about the business of teaching us how to sit.

Chiropractors talk about the business of teaching us how to stand.

Preachers are in the religion business.

Musicians are in the music business.

Pediatricians are in the baby business.

Cardiologists are in the heart business.

We have taken the world apart and put it back together again as a business.

The business of government.

The business of education.

The business of health.

The business of art.

We live the illusion that we understand what business is, when in fact we don't.

Despite what most people think, business isn't doing or creating something to be sold.

Business is a living thing which feeds and grows on the expectations, perceptions, needs, fears, and greed of the people with whom it comes into contact.

Business is a product of everything we believe to be true, need to be true, want to be true.

Our businesses are us.

❋ ❋ ❋ ❋

Which brings us to the point at hand: The Power Point and the Position of One.

That is that a business, any business, can only succeed to the degree that it gives each and every one of its Four Primary Influencers MORE than they can expect from any one of its competitors.

The way in which a business accomplishes this objective is what one would call a *good idea.*

An idea that will attract customers to it.

An idea that will attract employees to it.

An idea that will attract suppliers to it.

An idea that will attract lenders to it.

It is an idea which attracts with the greatest of force, the interest and attention of the Four Primary Influencers, and acts with the same force with which it attracts.

The force of any idea originates in the essential needs, perceived preferences, and unconscious expectations of the people it is intended to serve; an idea has no force of its own.

Thought of in that way, a good idea for a business is one which serves the most people best. And a bad idea for a business is one which serves the most people least.

The Power Point—the Position of One—is that locus of energy, that fusion of attention created when a good idea attracts to itself the self-interests of customers, employees, suppliers, and lenders alike with an equal, active, intensely interested force, which then moves out into the world to attract more force which, in turn, moves out into the world to attract even more force, thus growing and expanding and exploding with a power unrivaled by its competitors.

Like a star. Like the sun. Like the Position of One.

Like the Power Point in the eye of a storm.

2.
THE POWER POINT AND THE FIVE ESSENTIAL SKILLS

The real unknown
is an emotional
unknown. . . .
We awaken to
darkness.
—Jacob Needleman

If a good idea for a business is one which serves the most people best, then we in the United States have some soul-searching to do.

Because there's something missing in most of our businesses.

And that something is meaning.

For our failure to understand the true role business has come to play in our lives, for our failure to truly listen to the people we come into contact with, for our bias toward serving our own special interests, for our raw, insatiable drive to get the material MORE we all seem to be saying we need, it can't be denied that too many of our businesses have become killing fields of the spirit; they, like us, have missed the deeper message.

To truly soar, a business must mean more than just money, more than just "things," more than what's easy, more than careers, inventory, production statistics, ROI, automobiles, lipgloss, remodeled kitchens, Management by Objectives, pensions, profit sharing, "golden parachutes," and skin tight jeans.

To achieve some measure of greatness, a business must somehow rise above the one-dimensional symbols and empty rituals of our everyday flat-world existence.

To truly attract the greatest amount of force, the greatest attention—to fully seize its Power Point—the idea behind a business must strike much deeper.

It must strike our imagination.

It must touch a strong, resonant, and resilient chord in the hearts of all those people it is intended to serve.

It must use its energy in a profound, intelligent, and compassionate way.

It must reach beyond the trivial, the course, the ordinary, the mundane.

It must give us more life.

It must become a presence impossible to ignore.

It must become a place in which the most transient MORE, the most predictable MORE, the most superficial MORE, the most immediate MORE, the most trivial MORE is never enough.

It must become heroic in everything it does.

It must touch the dying part of each and every one of us and raise us to some higher place.

✳ ✳ ✳ ✳

Five essential skills are needed at the outset to create a great business. I say at the outset, for these skills must be in place if the idea for the business is to possess the size, the scale, the magnitude, the ecstatic quality—the power—needed to enter the race.

To some degree, every great business possesses these skills. I would go so far as to say that a business without them is dead.

❅ ❅ ❅ ❅

The first essential skill—the most fundamental of all—is *concentration.*

Concentration is the foundation upon which all right action in the world depends.

Without concentration a business will have no presence, no inner force, no magnetic center to which people, upon whom it depends for its life, energy, and force, will be attracted. Without concentration there is no ability to listen, to respond, to be available.

Concentration is not only something a great business must *do,* it is also the *result* of such doing; as a business concentrates its attention it also *becomes* concentrated, the convergent point to which energy is drawn, the Power Point.

A T'ai-chi master, T'an Meng-hsien, in his *Song of Central Equilibrium,* says:

> *We are centered, stable and still*
> *as a mountain.*
> *Our ch'i sinks to the tan-t'ien and*
> *we are as if suspended from above.*
> *Our spirit is concentrated within and*
> *our outward manner perfectly composed.*
> *Receiving and issuing energy are*
> *both the work of an instant.*

Said another way, a great business owns a place in the world.

It stands squarely in that place, but is able to move in an instant.

Its energy, its *ch'i,* flows without obstruction.

It is loose, flexible, and yet as solid as a mountain.

Its face looks within and without in the very same moment.

Its power is continuously in motion, yet, at the same time, infinitely still.

All are drawn to it as to a vision.

It does important things.

※　※　※　※

The second essential skill is *discrimination,* the ability to choose upon what, where, and whom our attention, our ability to concentrate, is directed.

If concentration provides us with the attention and energy we need, discrimination provides us with the intention, the will to select the most important work to do.

It is through discrimination that a business develops standards, both strategically, in the form of a mission, as well as tactically, in the form of behavior.

It is through the development of standards that a business develops discipline.

It is through the development of discipline that a business develops patience.

It is through the development of patience that a business develops vision.

It is through the development of vision that a business develops insight.

It is through the development of insight that a business develops conviction.

It is through the development of conviction that a business develops awareness.

It is through the development of awareness that a business develops empathy.

It is through the development of empathy that a business develops relationships.

It is through the development of relationships that a business develops more life.

※　※　※　※

The third essential skill is *organization,* the ability to turn chaos into order.

If concentration provides the energy and attention needed for right action to take place and discrimination provides the intention and standards needed to know what action needs to be taken, then organization provides the room for right action to take place.

There are three things which can be so organized: time, space, and work.

(Despite what many believe—and what most try to do—people cannot be organized. Only the work people do can be organized. All attempts to organize people instead of their work creates exactly the opposite of what organization is intended to do. Rather than order, it creates chaos. Rather than ease, it creates dis-ease. Rather than efficiency, it creates boredom. Rather than flexibility, it creates bureaucracy. Rather than room, it creates confinement.)

The organization of time prevents the overutilization of energy to achieve one's objectives; just enough time—and no more—within which the right action can be efficiently performed.

The organization of space produces the right tools in the right place in the right quantity to support the right action with an economy of effort.

The organization of work identifies the natural way to take action, the relationships between functions, and the coordination between the two.

When employed with skill, organization always produces a sense of great ease.

When employed unwisely, organization always produces resistance.

❋   ❋   ❋   ❋

The fourth essential skill, *innovation,* turns order into right action.

Innovation is sometimes called the "Best Way" skill; it is always in search of perfection.

While organization is interested in efficiency, innovation is concerned with effectiveness—faster, cheaper, smoother, softer.

Innovation is what children do all the time.

Like children, it is playful, bright, light, joyful.

Also like children, innovation is almost always irresponsible. Left to its own devices, it will almost always get itself into trouble.

It is always imagining new possibilities, and acting on such imagining.

It is willing to try anything once.

That is why without concentration, discrimination, and organization, innovation could very well sink the ship.

On the other hand, without innovation the ship wouldn't be very much fun.

❋ ❋ ❋ ❋

The fifth essential skill is *communication.*

It is the skill through which results are produced in the world.

It touches and is touched, reaches out and is reached for, moves and is moved upon, acts and is acted upon.

Communication is the channel through which life is conveyed.

Through which the energy of the idea is transmitted.

Through which the mind and the body and the spirit are merged and projected into a force for right action.

It is the medium through which attractions are formed, and then deepen.

It is the bond we each have with the world.

3.
THE POWER POINT MATRIX: THE FOUR CATEGORIES OF PREFERENCE

The constituents of matter and the basic
phenomena involving them are all interconnected,
interrelated, and interdependent; . . . they cannot
be understood as isolated entities, but only as
integrated parts of the whole.

—Fritjof Capra,
The Tao of Physics

On my sixteenth birthday, 38 years ago, I bought a very special car.

It was a 1947 Ford coupe.

I think of John Anderson, the man who sold it to me, as the quintessential entrepreneur.

Not that I thought of him like that at the time.

At the time I wasn't interested in business. I was simply a 16-year-old boy who was about to negotiate the most important decision of his life, and John Anderson was the man who was either going to make it possible or not.

In retrospect, I know that John Anderson was a business genius.

Whether by intention or not, he did every little thing right.

A few words about John Anderson.

He wasn't in business at all, but an engineer working at Lockheed.

I saw his small classified ad in *The Anaheim Bulletin,* announcing the fact that he had a 1947 Ford for sale.

The ad said, mysteriously: "Once you see it, you'll wonder why."

I called, scheduled an appointment for the following day after school, and then proceeded to climb the walls for 24 hours until the time came to see the car.

What I had failed to tell John Anderson over the phone was the fact that I had three seemingly insurmountable problems.

One, I hadn't told my folks that I was going to buy a car.

Two, I didn't have enough money to buy a car.

And, three, I absolutely couldn't live for another day without owning my own car!

It was with that knowledge festering inside of me that I nervously rang John Anderson's door bell that Thursday afternoon.

John Anderson opened the door.

He was a slim, tall, nondescript man with neatly cropped blond hair and bright blue, intelligent-looking eyes in his early 40s, although he looked much younger.

He was wearing a khaki shirt, open at the collar, and matching trousers. Both were starched and pressed with a military crispness.

His brown shoes gleamed.

He smiled warmly, shook my hand, invited me in, introduced me to his wife who was shelling peas at the kitchen table, and then led me out to the garage where he told me he kept the car.

The small, white, single-car garage stood separately from the house. I followed John Anderson to the garage door, and waited for what seemed like an eternity while he unlocked a large padlock secured to the door handle.

As though anticipating the question I didn't have the nerve to ask, he said: "I keep the door locked, just in case."

In case of what, I couldn't imagine. Until he opened the door.

Standing before us was the car, completely enclosed in a tight-fitting canvas tarp! The sole object in the garage, it sat frozen, as though hovering, in the space before me—a surprise waiting to be opened, a mystery waiting to be solved.

It was as if John Anderson had brought me to his garage to unveil a secret he had been hiding there for who knows how long—one he was about to share for the very first time, with me, and only me, his unwitting co-conspirator! It was almost more than I could bear.

"Would you like to help me take this off?" John Anderson asked as he moved to the front of the car, touching the canvas tarp lightly with his hand.

Was he kidding?

I mumbled something incoherent like, "Mmhm", and then waited for the instructions I knew would come. Instinctively I knew you didn't simply grab a tarp like this and dump it on the ground.

Fortunately, I didn't have to wait long.

"Just do exactly what I do." John Anderson said—as if I would have dared to do anything else!

He moved to the front right side of the car, motioned me to the rear right side of the car with a nod of his head, and then reached down and began to pull the tarp straight up overhead. I did the same.

Yet, as much as I wanted to follow his lead, I couldn't help but be distracted by what came into view.

The car absolutely glistened!

First came the chrome bumper, then the light grey rear fender, then the bright burnished red of the tail light.

Each, in turn, glistened with a luster of its own.

Each part accentuated the other, magnified the other, transformed the other, enriched the other. It was love at first sight!

I can see that '47 Ford coupe as clearly and as wonderfully today as I saw it that first time in John Anderson's garage. As we lifted the tan tarp up and over the roof, folding it as he indicated—like a flag—with loving, deliberate attention, we slowly revealed each part of the car: first the chrome bumper, then the grey fender, then the red tail light, the rear window, the roof, the trunk, the chrome trunk handle. Until, all at once, they merged into a whole car, a presence—a shining gift—better than I would have dared to imagine, better than I possibly could have conceived in my mind's eye.

After completing the folding, John Anderson took the tarp, opened the trunk of the car, laid the folded tarp down inside, softly but firmly closed the trunk door, and then stepped quietly aside where he stood waiting without saying a word.

I think I said, "Wow!" but I can't be sure. If I did, it was to myself. The car held me in thrall.

The white walls, the chrome hub caps, the deep, dark symmetrical tread of the tires, the windows, the chrome door handles, the fenders, the doors, the slow, lilting curve of the car itself—all came together into a luminescent statement about what a car could mean to a 16-year-old boy. More than anything I could have said, or John Anderson could have said, more than anything *anyone* could have said—this shimmering little Ford coupe, with its meticulous cleanliness, its deep sense of order, said it all.

Nothing could have been more to the point.

Nothing could have touched me any deeper.

The red, the grey, the chrome, the glass, the white and black rubber all coalesced into an exhilarating vision of an extraordinary machine which promised to take me away to places I had never been and had never imagined, and which would free me forever from the inhibiting binds of my 16-year-old body.

Then John Anderson said, "Let's go for a ride."

✳   ✳   ✳   ✳

There are four Categories of Preference which every business must satisfy in the minds and hearts of each of its four Primary Influencers.

Visual Preferences, Emotional Preferences, Functional Preferences, and Financial Preferences make up what I call the Power Point Matrix.

John Anderson intuitively understood this idea.

To John Anderson, the sale of his 1947 Ford coupe was much more than a commercial transaction. Indeed, the car itself was much more than a car.

To John Anderson, his 1947 Ford coupe was an *idea*.

And, the sale of his 1947 Ford coupe was therefore an extension of that idea.

As was John Anderson himself, as was I, and, without knowing it, as were to become my parents and John Anderson's wife. All of us were an extension of that idea, all of us influencers, all of us influenced, all of us possessing preferences which needed to be satisfied—*which would be satisfied*—for the idea to become action, for the idea to move into its future and find itself joined with the world. Visual Preferences, Emotional Preferences, Functional Preferences, Financial Preferences.

The idea of John Anderson's 1947 Ford coupe, held within it all of the possibilities which would unfold—possibilities which were already there at the instant of its conception.

Within that particular 1947 Ford coupe, resided the 16-year-old boy in both John Anderson and me, as well as, all mothers, all fathers, all wives.

Each of us loving it, hating it, needing it, avoiding it, wishing it, dreaming it, creating it, negating it, defending it, denying it, dreading it—*lusting after it*—along with our relationships with each other; our relationships with ourselves; our ideas of a car; our ideas of buying, selling, and money; our ideas of every single unavoidable and interdependent part of this complex, subtle, and hopelessly entangled web of interactions and contradictions among the thoughts, feelings, and flesh of virtual strangers.

This, after all, was—and is—what the game called *Business* is all about.

✳ ✳ ✳ ✳

What was to become and has remained in my mind and heart—a successful business transaction for both John Anderson and me—never could have happened had not John Anderson instinctively, yet unwittingly, used the Power Point Matrix in his relationship with himself, my parents, his wife, and me.

❋   ❋   ❋   ❋

As we drove, John Anderson talked.

"I guess you might say I have a passion for mechanical things. How they look; how they function; how they *exceed* their own limits; how they fit into the world. It's always been a passion of mine, for as long as I can remember."

He turned to look at me, "How about you, does any of this mean anything to you?"

"I don't know," I answered.

But what John Anderson was saying reminded me of my saxophone teacher more than anything else.

"You and Merle would really get along," I said to John Anderson. "I've never known anybody as interested as Merle is in how to make things work as well as they possibly can. He's an absolute genius when it comes to fine-tuning my saxophone. All the while I figure my horn's about as good as it'll ever get, and then Merle does something to it and it's a totally new horn! Is that what you mean?"

John Anderson was grinning from ear to ear.

"That's it exactly," he said. "That's what this car means to me. It's the perfect 1947 Ford coupe." If I wanted to buy a used car, I'd want it to look just like this. I'd want it to drive just like this. I'd want someone to have cared for it just like this—like it was the most important thing in the world. *Like whatever it could be, it was.*"

He turned down a quiet, tree-lined street, pulled up to the curb, and parked.

"Why don't you try it?" he said.

※　※　※　※

As I think back to it, it is as though I was fated to own John Anderson's car.

As though the ad in *The Anaheim Bulletin* had been a letter written directly to me.

As though the 1947 Ford coupe in John Anderson's garage was waiting just for me.

As though John Anderson knew that I would be the only one to call, the only one to show up at his door, and that I would be the only one to drive away in his car.

And that whatever needed to be done to accomplish that end, John Anderson would do, would handle, and would take responsibility for.

After driving the car back to his garage, replacing the tarp, and locking the garage door, John Anderson and I sat down at his kitchen table to talk business.

He never even asked me if I wanted to buy the car; it was a foregone conclusion!

Instead, we talked about my problems.

My parents, my money, and my need.

As we talked, a picture of the car waiting outside in the garage hovered in my mind.

As we talked, the feeling of the car's steering wheel lingered in my hands.

As we talked, I could feel the exhilarating sensation of driving quietly down the tree-lined street—in *my* car. I could see the fleeting, shimmering shadows of the leaves as they passed silently overhead—in *my* car. I could see the green lawns and pastel-colored houses sleepily drifting by on either side—in *my* car. I could see the crystal-clear gleam of the windshield, the soft grey sheen of the seats, and the deep burnished chrome dashboard John Anderson had had specially made—for *my* car.

As we talked, it was all over but the shouting.

※　※　※　※

John Anderson called my parents.

"It seems we have a problem." he said.

"Your son wants to buy my car, and I don't think we have a choice in the matter. But before we talk about it, I'd like for us to meet."

I could imagine my mother's dark worried frown at the other end of the phone, my father's usual uncontrollable anger at being trapped into a discussion he didn't want to have—didn't need at this time. I waited for the explosion. But, surprisingly, it didn't come. John Anderson listened quietly and attentively for a moment or two, nodded affirmatively a few times, agreed to something apparently suggested by my parents, and then hung up the phone.

They were coming over in 30 minutes and I was to wait for them.

※　※　※　※

Need I paint you a picture of my parents coming to John Anderson's door, of how weird I felt standing in the home of someone who, only two hours before, had been a literal stranger (but who now, in some odd and unfathomable way, had taken on the mantle of a surrogate father for the special ritual which was unfolding before us)? Need I describe waiting for my parents to say hello, to acknowledge my presence, waiting for the thunder of their terrible anger at being caught up in this drama to strike?

Need I paint you a picture of John Anderson's warm and respectful greeting—of the calm, gracious man my parents saw before them in his neat khaki clothes, in his neat and normal home, with his bright, yet very calm blue eyes?

Need I describe his wife, who by now had become a very real participant in this strangely natural unfolding event, smiling warmly in her living room, inviting my parents to take a seat, the coffee and cookies they shared together, with me hovering on the fringes of their conversation like some nervous, fretting, anxious, and pestering old bird?

Need I paint a picture for you of the eventual walk to the garage— that mysterious, wondrous place which I had first walked to only two hours before? Out of respect for John Anderson and out of tolerance for me, my parents were going to look at this car, this troublesome thing which had suddenly brought so much unneeded emotion and disorder to their lives!

Need we take in the surprise I saw on their faces (especially my father's), as they saw what I had seen waiting in the garage, and as my father awkwardly performed the ritual with John Anderson and the spotless tan tarp that I had performed so awkwardly only a short time before?

I had never seen the boy in my father's face until that moment, and I have never seen it since!

Need I take you on the unnecessary but inevitable ride the four of us took—like a hastily assembled family, my father too big and solid at the wheel for such an ephemeral occasion, John Anderson relaxed and smiling in the passenger's seat beside him, my mother and I sitting stiffly upright side by side in the small back seat like two dark birds on a telephone wire, staring straight ahead, afraid to look at each other for fear some spell might be broken and we would all suddenly and terribly disappear from the face of the earth. Such a strange and dreamy spectacle we must have seemed to people as we passed by on the road, as we carried out the many separate yet hyphenated steps of this extraordinary ritual. Need we go through each of those still, quiet, intense, vivid, and unforgettable moments which led us all remarkably and uncomplainingly to the very end— that invisible, magical, and seamless point at which the pieces of this extraordinary yet ordinary ritual finally joined together as naturally and as effortlessly as two velcro strips?

Need I say it? The deal was done!

❋ ❋ ❋ ❋

Visual Preferences, Emotional Preferences, Functional Preferences, Financial Preferences.

The potency and vitality of a business can only be actualized to the degree that it fills the possibilities to be discovered within each of these Categories of Preference as they are experienced by each of their four Primary Influencers.

If you do not believe me, see the car!

See the garage!

See John Anderson!

Feel the order, the control, the exquisite naturalness of this potentially disastrous event!

Everyone's preferences were served.

My parents', John Anderson's, his wife's, and mine.

We all got exactly what we needed—what we wanted.

It was a marvel of synchronicity.

Let's take a look at the Categories of Preference one at a time.

4.
THE FIRST CATEGORY OF PREFERENCE: THE VISUAL IDEAL

You never get a second chance to make a first impression.

—Anonymous

In "The Red Wheelbarrow," a poem by William Carlos Williams, he says:

> *so much depends*
> *upon*
>
> *a red wheel*
> *barrow*
>
> *glazed with rain*
> *water*
>
> *beside the white*
> *chickens.*

I first read that poem at least 30 years ago. But it wasn't until I found myself driving along a winding Sonoma County country road with a close friend on a rainy spring afternoon in 1969 that I fully appreciated it.

If you've never been there, the springtime hills in Sonoma County, California are like a rolling green sea. Nestled between the waves are small ranches, oak and eucalyptus trees, low-lying brush, and out-croppings of brown jagged rock.

We were driving along a narrow fence-lined road when we came to a sharp turn. Upon turning the corner, we suddenly came face to face with a scene so vivid, so striking, that I can clearly remember every part of it to this day.

It was a small, yellow ranch house, with bright green trim around the eaves and white molding around the windows and the door.

As we turned the corner, the sun came out from behind a storm cloud and struck the house, transforming it into a blaze of yellow light shot up from the ground and blinding me with its radiance. My friend must also have been temporarily blinded, because he slammed on the brakes and we skidded to a halt directly in front of the small house's fenced front yard.

Standing before us in the middle of the yard, halfway between the fence and the house, was a large, glowing, bright-red, meticulously cared for antique wagon. The drops of rainwater streaming down its sides glistened in the sun like diamonds.

But that wasn't all.

For surrounding the wagon was a yard full of pure white turkeys, their red wattles bobbing up and down!

Can you see it?

Can you feel it?

Can you hold this image in your mind? Do you wonder whose yard it is, and why the wagon, and had someone just fed the turkeys? What smells do you associate with this picture? What feelings come to mind? What thoughts arise from your past, from your imagination, from ideas you had about such things when you were a little boy or girl, or even now, as you are today?

Can you see how profoundly we're touched by such visual images?

It should become immediately obvious to you how important the conception, creation, and maintenance of a strong visual impression is to the ultimate success of a business.

A business, like a farm yard—like an old country road—is first and foremost a visual thing. What a business looks like communicates more about its thoughts, feelings, considerations, and intentions, more immediately and more lastingly—more *humanly*—to the people with whom it interacts than anything else that business can do!

As William Carlos Williams said, *"So much depends upon it!"*

And so much does.

For it is virtually impossible for anyone to see anything without drawing an instantaneous, if unconscious, conclusion about it.

In fact, it is not so much that we quickly draw conclusions about what we see, but that the conclusions we draw were already drawn long before we see it.

Each of us possesses (or, more accurately, is possessed by) a vast underground visual storehouse we call our *unconscious.*

This storehouse, our unconscious,—this picture book!—is bursting with a rich, complex assortment of visual symbols, associations, interpretations, judgements, meanings, feelings, and physical reactions—in short, conclusions—all of which conspire automatically with each other with laser-like speed, to shape our very existence.

What we wear, what we drive, where we work, where and how we live, what we think—the very objects, spaces, colors, distances, forms, and people we surround ourselves with, and by which we're surrounded—are all significant parts of this extraordinarily complex web of visual conclusions each of us has formed.

A mother nursing her child, a grandmother preparing the thanksgiving turkey for her grown-up children and her grandchildren, a young father roughhousing with his son and their labrador retreiver in the backyard, that same man, grown grey, showing his grandson how to tune up a carburetor in a period truck, a tall distinguished man in an impeccably tailored dark navy blue suit, waiting outside of a contemporary office building—all are pictures, visual representations of deeply held conclusions we all have made some time in our lives. They may even be representative of Jung's archetypes—pictures we all share, pictures which touch us all in much the same way. And there are an infinite number of such pictures, waiting to be understood, waiting to be identified, but working unconsciously in each and every one of us in the same way. No matter what any of us thinks, they shape our lives!

Do you see what I mean? Do you understand the importance of this concept?

So much depends upon it!

If all that we see touches us so immediately, so completely, if every visual impression we receive causes each of us to feel, think, and act in a certain pre-programmed—if not totally predictable—way (and it does!), is it any wonder then that the conception, creation, and maintenance of the visual impression of a business is so critical to its success?

Should it come as such a surprise to you when I say that to conceive, create, and successfully maintain an extraordinarily effective business—a Power Point business—has much more to do with the management of *impressions* than it has to do with the management of people?

The management of impressions *is* the management of people.

And visual impressions are the most powerful impressions of all.

※ ※ ※ ※

The problem seems to be that the vast majority of businesses in this country—small or large—simply don't get it, or what's worse, simply don't care.

The "search for excellence" in theory seems somehow to have eluded us in practice.

Contrary to popular belief, there's an overwhelming poverty of the entrepreneurial spirit in this country.

Walk or drive down just about any business street, or walk inside just about any business you choose, and you'll immediately be accosted by the visual symptoms of our entrepreneurial malaise.

Signs, windows, sidewalks, buildings, trucks, employees' dress, bathrooms, floors, countertops, aisles, walls—rundown, dirty, worn out, unimaginative, decaying, cluttered, confusing—a visual mess!—businesses disintegrating right before our eyes.

Yet, all those signs were new once, all the windows newly installed, all the floors, the walls, the bathrooms, the desks, the file cabinets, the trucks, the automobiles, the forklifts, the merchandise racks, every single element of every business was at the outset a function of someone's dream. What happened? What stopped working? What do people think as they go to work there, as they buy there? *What are the owners thinking?*

I believe it could be proven that a visually deteriorating business is the act of an emotionally deteriorating mind.

What do people feel as they are visually accosted every day of their lives by all of this negativity, neglect, and disinterest?

Well, let me tell you a story.

It's about two brothers who own a great store.

Not that it was always a great store—it wasn't.

Indeed, if you had seen it when I first saw it, you'd have to agree with me that in Marty and Sol Weissberg's business a visual renaissance has taken place.

"A transformation," Marty calls it.

"A miracle," says Sol.

But whatever you'd call it, it happened this way.

❋ ❋ ❋ ❋

In 1983, Marty Weissberg was called home from graduate school at the University of San Francisco to help his older brother, Sol, run the family business after their father, Morris, died unexpectedly at a young 53.

Fortunately for both of them, the business, Weissberg's Army-Navy, sort of ran itself, if in a lackluster way.

Customers came and went; employees too. Nobody seemed to know why.

Although Sol and Marty had both served their apprenticeship in the business from the ages of eight and ten respectively, most of their time had been spent at their father's beck and call, unpacking the green, grey, blue, brown, and black military merchandise which arrived in enormous brown cardboard boxes from who-knew-where, and pricing it according to their father's cryptic, hand-printed instructions, using a pricing strategy only Morris understood. They then stacked the merchandise on the already jam-packed shelves, and hung it on the special racks which their father ordered them to move around the store at what were apparently strategically significant times of the week or the month—from the back of the store to the front, to either the right side or the left, down the middle aisle or by the cash register, to the sidewalk on clear sunny days, and ceremoniously labeled SALE in bright red bold letters, (even though both Marty and Sol knew that the prices hadn't been changed). They swept the floors, threw out the trash, cleaned the windows, and occasionally—only occasionally— were entrusted to "work with the customers" who their father seemed to *know* wouldn't buy, and rarely did. Morris dealt with all the rest.

Unfortunately—and despite the long, dreary, chore-full hours they spent in the store after school and on weekends for most of their adolescent years—neither Marty nor Sol "knew the business," as their father was given to say. Morris was so busy working the store, doing business, getting by as best as his wits would allow him to, that he had never gotten around to teaching it to them.

And then he died, and the store was theirs—a business both Marty and Sol hated, not only for all the time it had taken from them as boys, but for their inability—now that they could be finally free of it once and for all—to say goodbye to it, to let go of it, to get rid of it forever, and finally to get on with the purpose of their individual lives.

Perhaps that was it, there was no purpose.

Just as when they were boys, their lives now seemed to be rolling along a track laid down by some unknown but implacable force pushing them from behind, a force which they had thought was Morris in the early years, until now, after Morris was gone, and no longer pushing and prodding and bullying them along—when they had no more excuses—here they were, still moving down the track, like mechanical men, like sleep-walkers, like two men with no thoughts, no life, no purpose of their own.

To Marty and Sol, if there was a life other than the business, they didn't know what it was. So they lived the only one they knew.

※   ※   ※   ※

Anyone who has grown up and taken over the reins of a family business (or a business ruled by a strong hand like Morris', whether a relative or not), knows what Marty and Sol were feeling.

It's like wearing someone else's suit. No matter how well it fits, it's never your own. The shoulders don't hang right, the pockets feel used by someone else's hands, the pants pull just a little bit here, sag just a little bit there, and when you stand in front of a mirror it isn't you standing there, it's only partly you. You can almost see the previous owner's face staring back!

Unfortunately, it's been my experience that few such heirs ever grow beyond that feeling of excruciating discomfort.

The suit never becomes theirs, no matter how much they wear it.

The business continues to look, act, and feel like the person who originally shaped it.

Despite its new tenant, the business continues to live a life all its own.

※ ※ ※ ※

For the first six months or so, Sol and Marty glowered at each other across distances of their own making, repeating in silence the dreary rituals of their boyhoods past.

But now, without their father to goad them on, the rituals were even more lifeless than before.

No Morris was there to tell them to move the racks.

No Morris was there to remind them to paint the red SALE signs.

No Morris exhorted them to sweep the floors, to take out the trash, to wash the windows and then—*remember*—to scrape them dry with the red rubber wiper on the long aluminum pole standing alone at the inside of the front door hanging down from a rack Morris made especially for that purpose.

No, there was no Morris there to do it, so Sol did it.

He did the only thing he could think to do.

He became Morris.

He became the father the two of them had lost.

One day he was Sol, the next day, Morris.

It was like a hunger had seized him.

He began to spend long hours after the store was closed and Marty had gone home, rummaging through his father's effects, seeking out clues, a trail, a sign, which could teach him what his father never did, which could teach him what his father knew.

Now, rather than simply copying the prices from old labels on new ones (as he and Marty had mechanically resorted to doing without Morris' notes and reminders to guide them), Sol began to make a study of Morris' arcane pricing logic by scrutinizing all the old pricing notes Morris had saved over the years, carefully comparing the notes to the purchasing invoices, the season, and then to the books, and noting the correlation between prices, purchases, seasons, and sales.

He discovered something any experienced retailer could have told him in a quick minute, but to Sol it was like an enormous cloud had been lifted from in front of his eyes.

He suddenly knew something his father had never taught him—he suddenly knew the secret behind doing business at Weissberg's Army-Navy.

He suddenly knew for the very first time what made the business tick.

And just as suddenly, he now knew for the very first time what it meant to own something all his own.

He also knew now why his father had kept it a secret.

And just as his father had before him, Sol now kept the secret from Marty.

❄   ❄   ❄   ❄

But, Sol could have saved himself the trouble.

For, just as Sol was going through his metamorphosis, Marty was privately going through one of his own.

Just as Sol was beginning to experience the freedom to become the father who had oppressed him, Marty was beginning to awaken to the exhilarating possibility that he was now, finally, free to become himself.

A new light in Marty was beginning to form.

You could see it in his eyes.

❄   ❄   ❄   ❄

A friend of mine who worked closely with Walt Disney for more than fifteen years, related to me what it was that made Walt Disney a special man to all those who worked with him.

"He had the innate ability to see things whole in a completely original way," my friend said.

"Where everyone else in a meeting would be caught up in specifics, Walt could *see* the finished product, he could envision what everyone else seemed to miss—the magic which lived within every project just beneath the surface, waiting to be discovered."

"That's where Walt lived," my friend told me, "in the magic beneath the surface of things. And only when he revealed what he saw there did it become obvious to everyone else *that it was there all the time.*"

That, I might suggest, is also where Marty Weissberg in his own small, but to me not insignificant, way was beginning to live—beneath the surface of things.

Indeed, I believe that it is there, *beneath* the surface of things, where the surface, the true reality, actually resides.

And so it is that the Visual Preference is so immediately critical to the success of a business.

For it is on the surface of the things we surround ourselves with that we reveal what we see things to be.

❃   ❃   ❃   ❃

Time wore on at Weissberg's Army-Navy.

As Sol grew more entrenched in the business, Marty grew even more detached.

As Sol spent more and more of his time recreating the past, Marty spent more and more of his time looking at the present.

As Sol became more and more consumed by the details of running the business as his father had before him, Marty became more and more consumed by the changes going on inside him.

The two brothers spent as little time talking to each other as possible. A deep gulf opened up between them.

To Sol, Marty was just "hanging around."

To Marty, Sol was going crazy.

But all the while, the business remained the same.

Weissberg's Army-Navy remained Weissberg's Army-Navy.

It was like nothing had happened since Morris died.

The business didn't know he had passed on.

The customers who only bought from Morris either went away or now bought from Sol.

Others replaced them. Indistinguishable people. People who came and went, said hello, said goodbye, exchanging their money for the goods that Sol, like his father before him, bought from sources Marty wasn't interested in, to arrive in large brown boxes as they always had, off the backs of trucks which came from who-knew-where, to be unpacked, labeled, and shunted around to the shelves and racks that had been there as long as Marty could remember, and, as far as Marty could tell, would be there for as long as Sol had his way.

To Marty, it wasn't so much that Sol was going crazy, though he certainly was, it was that Sol was on a track of his father's choosing, and he didn't even know it; he couldn't see it; he didn't seem to care.

To Marty, it was obvious that Sol was slowly but surely being sucked down into the suffocating quicksand of their boyhood past. The store was consuming Sol, just as it had their father! This store—the same store his father had slaved away in for as long as Marty could remember, the same store in which he and Sol had wasted their childhood years, the same store that he, Marty, somehow couldn't, for lack of anything better to do, get away from today—this store was doing what it always had done, was simply doing what he had always remembered it doing.

So what was so wrong with that?

It was only then that it came to Marty, that it hit him square between the eyes. It was only then that Marty clearly saw, as though for the very first time, what had *always* been there, had haunted him throughout his childhood, had clung to him like an oppressive grey fog as he left school every day on his way to the store, had laid there waiting for him like that enormous, grotesque Sumatran Toad he had once seen at the Zoo, squatting motionless as a stone in its small glass aquarium, its mottled, brown, lumpy skin glistening malevolently in the sweating, green-grey, tropical light—*it was all so ugly!*

From the front of the store, with its faded red neon letters spelling out the family name in belligerent block letters 14 feet long and 4 feet high across the squat, square face of the old brick building, to the inside of the store, with its low, brown tin ceiling and its rows of fluorescent lights, which could never brighten the darkness of the store beneath them; from the black, perennially soiled linoleum floors, the grey metal racks with their squeaky rubber wheels, and the rows of dark metal shelves, to the hand-lettered signs hanging from the ceiling telling the customers where to find—among the bewildering array of sloppily stacked merchandise—the pants, jackets, boots, socks, belts, knives, canteens, shirts, hats, tents, sleeping bags, mosquito nets, socket wrenches, and all the other exotic military paraphenalia known as *surplus*—it all displayed a blatant lack of attention, of care, of imagination, of interest!

And then there was the back of the store: the massive, rusted, steel-framed doors; the thick, scarred, ancient planks of the floor and loading dock, stained black from years of abuse; the swollen, cracked, and tortured asphalt of the narrow, twisting alley with its ever-present trash, broken bottles, over-flowing garbage cans, and sagging chain link fences running between the dark-stained brick back walls of the neighboring stores.

Finally, there was the bathroom: small and dank, like a cold, sweaty closet, with its unpainted concrete floor, both the wash bowl and toilet stained and streaked after years of use; with its solitary, naked 100-watt bulb hanging down from the impenetrable shadows above, the only other light coming from a small window above the sink, barred against forceable entry, (as though anyone would want to break in there!). The whole room was filthy from years of neglect; the dirt, the cobwebs, and whatever other undescribable blight had risen from the alley behind the store had crusted over the window and cast a yellow, spotted pall over the peeling, damp brown door and walls.

As a boy, Marty would do anything other than go to the bathroom in that store, and when he finally couldn't wait any longer, he'd go down the street to the gas station at the corner where at least it was clean!

At last, Marty fully understood what it was about the store that so deeply depressed him.

Despite what Marty had always believed to be true about his father— that he loved nothing else but his business, that he cared for nothing else but the store—Marty now knew that exactly the opposite was true.

He knew that the store had so angered Morris—so infuriated him, so consumed him—that there was simply nothing left for anyone, or anything, else.

It wasn't the fact that *he* hated the store that depressed Marty so much, but that his *father* had!

The ugliness of Weissberg's Army-Navy was a mute, but eloquent, testament to the fact that his father felt himself—and then became—a prisoner there, until the only way out was to die.

✻ ✻ ✻ ✻

So that was the madness that Marty saw in Sol's eyes.

Like his father before him, Sol too had become a prisoner of the store. Like his father before him, the store enraged Sol. Like his father before him, the store became Sol's justification for not living. For both Morris and now Sol, the store had become the ugly fact of their absence of love for what they were doing and of the life they had both given up to do it.

And, like Morris, Sol mistakenly thought that by possessing the store, by owning it—*by keeping it his secret*—he could ultimately get even.

Only Marty knew different.

❈   ❈   ❈   ❈

At Disneyland, it costs the company an estimated $150,000 a year just to steam clean the streets! Not to mention all the other countless daily details of preparing the park—the gardens, the restaurants, the thousands upon thousands of uniforms, the myriad other minute and seemingly infinite number of small, insignificant tasks associated with the visual preparation of Disneyland for every day the park opens for business, just as Walt had envisioned it in his dream of the business back at the beginning when most people thought him to be crazy ("You want to do *what?*"), when the park was just an outsized, elaborate, and insane idea, which, according to common business wisdom at the time (and at this time, and for all times it seems), could never be justified economically, it was that idealistic.

And again, at McDonald's, it costs the company an estimated $250 a day to prepare each one of their 11,200 stores for the next day's 22 million customers and their 159,000 employees—a corporate commitment of over $2.8 million *a day* to the ordinary (at McDonald's, made extraordinary) daily ritual of visually preparing the floors, the equipment, the windows, the parking lots, the sidewalks, the signage, the counters, the uniforms, and the equipment—all the unavoidable and integral parts of the visual integrity of the McDonald's corporate image as imagined by its founder, Ray Kroc, at the very outset of the business when he had crew people clean up all litter within a block of each restaurant!

And yet again, at Federal Express, it costs the company an estimated $26,000 a day to steam wash their 22,000 internationally recognized red, violet, and white trucks to make certain that the company maintains its visual impact as it was envisioned on the rich entrepreneurial drawing board of Fred Smith's inspired mind, long before the business began, long before the first truck rolled out the door.

❈   ❈   ❈   ❈

Marty and I talked about the miraculous transformation of his and Sol's business.

"I swear," Marty said to me, "It struck me just like that."

"As suddenly as my father died, I just as suddenly came alive."

He continued, a dark light growing in his eyes.

"There was the mourning period, of course, even though I didn't realize that's what I was doing at the time.

"Of course, Sol and I mourned in different ways. To Sol, mourning was an act of honoring the past. He felt somehow that he had let our father down, that he had disappointed him, that if he had taken a more active interest in the business our father wouldn't have died. So he was literally compelled to act out every little thing my father did, exactly as my father would have done it.

"To me," Marty continued, "mourning was an act of greiving for my lost childhood, the games I never played, the playing we never did as a family, the lack of pure joy in our life.

"At first I thought it was just Sol who was going crazy. But, then I came to realize that we both were. But, of course, we had no choice. Our father was a lunatic. He raised us to be lunatics. We were simply acting out his wishes.

"But, gradually, deep in my heart, I began to feel a sharp, aching, almost unbearable pain for the extraordinary price my father had made Sol and me pay as children, the loss of joy, the loss of imagination, the loss of curiosity, of color, of vitality, of creativity, the loss of our childhood, the loss of ourselves.

"I swear I carried the pain of that loss around with me every day, from the day I came home to the store after my father died, to the day that the light turned itself on in my heart.

"And, suddenly, I found myself free, not as a 24-year-old man, but as a boy! It suddenly became clear to me, not so much something I thought, but in a burst of feeling so strong, so deeply compelling, that I began to sob uncontrollably. I must have cried for hours.

"This might sound stupid to you," Marty said to me, almost apologetically, as though what he was about to say would be impossible for me to understand, "But, it was like I fell in love with myself as a boy. It was like I had, in an instant, become both the father I wish I had had, and the boy I wish I could have been, and it was like the father I had now become touched me, his son, and said, 'Trust your heart, whatever you need to do, do it, don't wait, there's time enough to die, I love you.'"

Marty continued, almost in a whisper, tears welling in his eyes, "At that moment, I loved my father more than I could ever remember. I could finally cry for him, for the loss of *his* childhood, for the terrible price he had paid for being a prisoner in a prison of his own making. God, how desperate he must have been."

He was quiet for a moment, and then went on.

"And when that happened, when I was reunited with myself, with this strange but wonderful little boy I had been, I finally realized that I was suddenly free to do anything I wished with the store. I could sell it. I could give it away. I could give my share to Sol. I could even *burn it down* if I wanted. Morris was gone. The prison door was open. There was no track to follow but my own. I didn't need permission anymore!"

*   *   *   *

The visual transformation of a business is an emotional thing, it comes best from the heart. It is a creation which when done exceedingly well is always endowed with a pure passion to touch something beyond the ordinary—the most human of expressions, a statement of dignity, of caring, of consideration, but most of all, of love.

It has less to do with the business as a commercial enterprise than it has to do with the business as a *human* enterprise—its relationship with people, their ideas, and the things that connect people and their ideas with the world around them.

In this regard, the business doesn't only produce products, but becomes *itself* the product of the people by whom and for whom it is created.

To effectively differentiate the business-as-a-product from all other businesses, a business must be a visual interpretation of a specific and well-thought-out point of view or philosophy regarding the questions we humans have asked of ourselves since time immemorial—questions of freedom, of God, of law, of integrity, of purpose, of loyalty, of service, of honor, of order, of beauty, of self-respect and respect for others, and many more.

In short, to rise above the ordinary, a business must become a visual statement of belief, of meaning—a medium through which people communicate with each other about what they believe in, what they care for, what is important to them.

Taken to that level, the visualization of a business is an art form.

And just like a work of art, there are at least six tangible components which comprise the Visual Matrix which need to be considered in the construction of a business.

These six components are *color, form, scale, order, detail,* and *information.*

※   ※   ※   ※

Color is the first thing people see, and is therefore a critical component of the Visual Matrix. What colors will best communicate the purpose of the business? Is the business playful? Is it serious? Is it up-beat? Is it formal? Is the business intended to touch the hearts of people, just their minds, or both their hearts and minds?

When I say "playful," do certain colors come to mind? When I say "somber" do you see the dark colors it evokes? When I say "up-beat," can you visualize what up-beat colors might be? Can you hear the *sounds* such colors make?

Form follows color in the order of importance. What form does the business take—from the logo, to the style of dress, to the architecture, to the products? Is it bold, adventurous, sedate, austere, comfortable, or powerful? Does it call for rounded, soft edges or sharp, angular edges? Or are there few edges at all? Can you imagine in your mind's eye what form a comfortable business might take? Do you remember the old yellow ranch house, with its small flock of white turkeys, and its antique red wagon? Was that comfortable, or was it adventurous? Can you imagine Thanksgiving in such a place? The family around the table, grandma in her wire-rimmed glasses, granddad grinning at his youngest grandson who is sitting in his highchair and throwing food across the table, everyone chattering, about the past, the present, the future, food steaming and plentiful on the huge dining room table? Comfortable? Austere? Sedate? Powerful? When you know what you wish to communicate in your business, the form will almost immediately appear.

Third in the Visual Matrix is *scale.* And what of the scale of the business? Is it built for people, or is it built to intimidate people? Does it take the breath away, or does it make us laugh? Does it say "this is going to be one hell of a time," as Disneyland says, stretching out as it does as far as the eye can see, or does it confine us so that we simply want to get out? Is it the scale of a gothic church, or of a miniature railroad? A gothic church is not built for comfort; a miniature railroad does not convey power.

Fourth in the Visual Matrix is *order.* Order is such a critical component of the visual business that I am continually amazed at how oblivious most businesses seem to be to the price they pay every single day for ignoring it. Order is just what it says: it is all things in their place; it is cleanliness; it is impeccability; it is a deep abiding sense of control—that there is a logic, a sensitivity, a commitment to keeping the jungle out of the clearing; it is a belief in the special quality of human life; it is the meticulous attention paid to maintenance—to the surface of things, of sustaining the newness, the freshness, the essence of things as we envisioned them new. Order is preparing the ground before us as though God himself were to visit.

Fifth in importance is *detail.* Once one has walked in the door, once one takes a closer look, it is detail which people begin to see, the shining copper rivets, exactly placed, 2 inches apart on the aluminum wastebasket; the specially designed pin with the company's logo on it on the blouse of every woman employee. Detail is the care one puts into all the little things of the business, so as people look closer they are continuously surprised by what they find.

And sixth, is *information.* Every business must find a visual way to transmit information to its customers, its employees, its suppliers, and its lenders—the information they each perceive they need—in the most visually compelling way possible. A small business consulting firm covers its reception area walls with "Impact Reports"—letters from its clients—telling the world how their business is improving. A pet store places charmingly informative picture cards next to each cage, describing the inhabitant's traits as a pet, as well as where they came from, what they eat, whether they are good for children, and the amount of care they require. An auto body shop provides its customers with a large glass window looking onto the shop floor, where its employees go about their specialized tasks in uniforms and with equipment color-coded by function, while an audio tape describes what the customer is watching.

Of course there are options in all of this.

Whether it be a meat market, a grocery store, a semiconductor plant, a church, or Weissberg's Army-Navy, the visualization of a business either can be reduced to the merely pragmatic, or raised to the ideal. It can be ordinary or sublime.

But it is certain that the higher one reaches the more power one feels.

✳︎ ✳︎ ✳︎ ✳︎

It wasn't easy, but Marty and Sol began to talk.

At first, Sol reminded Marty of Morris. He got angry, he stormed away to his office. He'd stay hunkered down at his desk for days.

But, gradually, over a period of several months, as Marty described it, "Morris finally let go of him."

"The truth was," Marty went on, "that Sol and I had more in common with each other than we ever did with our father."

They began to talk.

They began to share.

They began to feel what it was like to be brothers.

At long last the gulf between them vanished, and Marty told Sol what he had in mind.

"I want this place to become a place of light," Marty said.

"I want people to come from all over town just to see it, whether they buy something or not.

"I want to put in a small restaurant, a coffee shop, and an indoor playground for little kids to play in while their parents walk around the store, with someone to watch them and take care of them for as long as their parents want. I want there to be a small stream running through the playground, with a waterfall roaring down from the ceiling. And I want Koi fish—golden and white and black spotted Koi—swimming in the stream, with green plants, and a place for the kids to feed the fish three times a day, and a small petting zoo, with lambs, and pygmy goats, and miniature horses. I want the place to be bright, and open, and colorful, and most of all I want it to be clean, spotless, absolutely perfect. I want it to be fun too. I want people to love being here—our employees, and our customers, and you, Sol, and me. I want to tear out the ceiling and go straight up to the roofjoists to give us some room to breath! I want to tear out the wall board, and sandblast the brick walls until they're absolutely new, bright red and white. I want to tear up the linoleum, and lay down thin strips of clear white oak, intermixed with brick and flag-stone paths leading to the garden at the base of the waterfall. I want to have bright grass-green antique benches located throughout the store, so that if people want to take a load off their feet, they can. I want there to be music, not *Muzac,* but real music, a live piano, or a string quartet, and sometimes, just for the hell of it, a small rock band, to give the place a kick in the ass! I want to market *colorful* products, no more dark blue, black, green, grey and brown, but bright blue, and red, and yellow, and green, and products for camping, hiking, fishing, hunting, all outdoor recreation and sports. And I want them to be displayed colorfully, dramatically, with big colorful plastic keys given to each customer when they walk in the door to use in video terminals to provide them with all the information they'll need about the more difficult to understand products, so that they'll never have to ask anyone where anything is, or what it does, or what the difference is between one product or another. Can you see it, Sol? And that's only the beginning. I want this place to shine! And I want something grand, something absolutely astonishing, something totally unexpected and stunning suspended from the ceiling by invisible wires to swoop down on the customers as they walk in the front doors. Perhaps one month it will be a giant glider, or another month a real bi-plane, or—even better—how about an incredible true-to-life model of an American bald eagle with 18 foot wings stretched out on either side, staring down at everyone with its huge, sharp yellow, eagle eyes! And, most of all, Sol, I want to change our name and the face of the building, and I want the sign to soar up from the roof so that no one can possibly miss it. And I want the sign to say: FLY-ING HIGH & FIELDSTONE GREEN!''

Marty reached behind him, took out a large brown paper wrapped package, tore it open, and turned the art board within it around so that Sol could see.

Sol stared at the illustration and blinked twice before saying, "But, what does it *mean?*"

Marty began to laugh, and then to roar, holding his sides, tears welling from his eyes.

"It means, old buddy, things are about to change."

5.
THE SECOND CATEGORY OF PREFERENCE: THE EMOTIONAL IDEAL

Man is a rope stretched between the animal and the Superman—a rope over an abyss. A dangerous crossing, a dangerous wayfaring, a dangerous looking-back, a dangerous trembling and halting.
—Thus Spake Zarathustra

To become a Power Point business, it is essential for a business to become a visual production. But for the production to have meaning, for the form to have substance, the Second Category of Preference, the Emotional Ideal, is equally essential, lest the production degenerate into what might be called visual rhetoric, "full of sound and fury, signifying nothing."

In a September, 1990 article in *Newsweek,* an Israeli General, Avigdor Kahalni, spoke to the question of combat in the desert, how to be victorious should the United States find itself in open conflict with the Iraquis.

My advice to the American troops in Saudi Arabia is simply this: don't waste valuable time on just getting comfortable; sleep six hours a day; drink plenty of water and use every other minute for training, training, training.

Fighting in the desert, surrounded by nothingness, a man runs the risk of losing sight of why he's there, except to survive. A soldier's motivation becomes doubly important. I believe the U.S. officers in Saudi Arabia should take the time now to sit with their men, to explain goals, to know every soldier personally, to give them the feeling they are the best, that their mission is a must. Leadership is at a premium in the desert, and without that nothing will be achieved.[1]

It might be argued that the comparison between war and business is an unreasonable one, that war brings with it a special edge, a unifying principle, that is impossible to sustain in an ordinary business engaged in mundane commercial transactions where life and death is not a day-to-day question, if a question at all.

I believe the opposite to be true.

I believe a great business becomes so to the degree that, like war, it raises serious questions. It brings us face to face with our own mortality. If there are no extrahuman challenges, it creates them and engages with its own resistance to change the desert of its own doubt. It forms its people into squads, and companies, and regiments, and batallions, and divisions and determines where the enemy is (it is always within), and launches, time and time again, into battle after battle, if only to take one yard at a time, to experience not so much the land that is acquired (although, of course, there is that), but the extraordinary inner strength that is developed, the camaraderie, the passion that is shared, passed on, handed from person to person, from heart to heart, a sense of purpose, of value, of being as fully human as we can be, given our limited understanding, our limited skill, our limited interest.

In his book, *The Master Game,* Robert S. De Ropp says:

What people really need and demand from life is not wealth, comfort or esteem but *games worth playing.* He who cannot find a game worth playing is apt to fall prey to *accidie,* defined by the Fathers of the Church as one of the Deadly Sins, but now regarded as a symptom of sickness. Accidie is a paralysis of the

1. *Newsweek,* November 9, 1990.

will, a failure of the appetite, a condition of generalized boredom, total disenchantment—"God, oh God, how weary, stale,
flat and unprofitable seem to me all the uses of this world!" Such
a state of mind . . . is a prelude to what is loosely called "mental
illness," which . . . fills half the beds in hospitals and makes
multitudes of people a burden to themselves and to society.
. . . Seek, above all, for a game worth playing. Such is the advice
of the oracle to modern man. Having found the game, play it
with intensity—play as if your life and sanity depended on it.
(They *do* depend on it.) Follow the example of the French exis-
tentialists and flourish a banner bearing the word "engagement."
Though nothing means anything and all roads are marked "NO
EXIT", yet move as if your movements had some purpose. If life
does not seem to offer a game worth playing, then *invent one*.
For it must be clear, even to the most clouded intelligence, that
any game is better than no game.[2]

"What is a game?" De Ropp asks. "It is essentially a trial of strength
or a trial of wits played within a matrix which is defined by rules.
Rules are essential. If the rules are not observed, the game would
cease to be a game at all. A meaningful game of chess would be
impossible if one player insists on treating all pawns as queens."

De Ropp goes on to say that the only game worth playing is what
he calls, "the Master Game," the aim of which is "true awakening,
full development of the powers latent in man."

※　※　※　※

Most of the people I know are not confused enough.

Oh, certainly, they would all admit to a certain degree of frustration,
doubt, a lack of certainty as to how a particularly vexing problem
could best be solved.

2. Robert S. De Ropp. *The Master Game*. New York: Dell, 1974.

Like how to get Jack to show up for work on time.

Or how to get the landlord to fix the air conditioner which, no matter what we say or do, blasts on at the coldest time of the day, and blasts off at the warmest.

But, aside from these petty frustrations which manage to bollix up our day from time to time, to my way of thinking none of that is what I would call a true confusion.

A true confusion means total disorientation.

Most of the people I know are pretty certain about where they stand on any subject, such as, "The dummies should be shot!" or "Anyone with an ounce of brains knows that a Chevy outperforms a Ford," or, "Mary should *never* wear brown. She looks like a damned wheat field gone to seed for God's sake. What's that girl thinking about?"

It is by taking a position on a subject, that most people immediately confirm they're alive: "Yoo-hoo, I'm here. That's me who said that."

Most people I know live moment to moment, state to state, voicing their opinions on just about everything, and, in the process, confirming their existence—the certainty of themselves. We all do it. It's a matter of habit. How else would we get on in life?

But, what I'm saying is that most of the people I know are not confused enough.

Because they rarely stop to see how little they actually *do* know—about anything—they rarely, if ever, put themselves into question.

They rarely, if ever, get to the point where they suddenly feel totally stupid.

Indeed, they rarely, if ever, allow themselves to feel stupid because it's not only scary to feel that way, to see how absolutely stupid we all are concerning just about everything, but it's drop-dead terrifying to come face to face with the dark, deep abyss of how little we actually know, and, even worse, with the alarming, unsettling, absolutely devastating, fact that most of the time *we're not even here.*

If we are to be honest with each other, we would have to agree that most people are like that.

Most people you know and most people I know.

In fact, if we really want to be honest with each other, if the truth was really to be revealed—*you and I are like that.*

Oh, yes we are. We're all certifiable dummies.

And what's worse, we're all mainly gone, absent, asleep, out to lunch most of the time, habit-ridden, doing an automatic dance of someone else's choosing, and—just like Marty and Sol—pushed along from behind.

It's my contention that if we were working in a great business, *someone would be telling us that all the time.*

Someone would be reminding us that we're not confused enough.

That we have too many stupid answers, and not enough questions, occupying our minds.

※　※　※　※

A great business, a Power Point business, makes it its business to keep *everyone* awake, its customers, its employees, its suppliers, and its lenders.

True, it's a difficult, often treacherous, path to take.

Because most people don't like to be confused; they don't like to be jostled; they don't like to feel jarred; they don't like to have someone say, "Think!" as Tom Watson at IBM was given to do; and they like to have opinions about everything that goes on. Don't we? Don't we all like that, honest to God, deep down inside, don't we all like to be *authorities?!*

On the other hand, isn't there a part of us, however small and timid, that loves to be shaken?

For it's that shock to awaken, it's that cosmic rap on the noggin, it's that existential kick in the ass, it's that primordial shout from our struggling old conscience which says, "Wake up! Wake up! Wake up!", that lifts us out of the ether, that snaps us out of our lockstep, that pins us to the wall of our sleep, and makes us look at it, makes us open our eyes, makes us breathe, think, move, *come alive!*

✳ ✳ ✳ ✳

I had a saxophone teacher once. As I mentioned earlier, his name was Merle.

Merle was a tyrant, a tormentor.

Other than the fact that he was a genius at the saxophone, he had nothing else going for him.

Merle must have weighed at least 300 pounds. He had a drinking problem too. Not that I ever saw him drunk, though I don't think I would have known it if he was. I was only nine years old when I started studying with him. But, at each one of my hour-long Saturday morning lessons—there were at least 400 of them in all, I studied with him for almost eight years—he drank down a whole quart of beer! Now, I know he had other students than me, about seven every day. That means that Merle drank at least seven quarts of beer a day for the entire time I knew him, and not once did I see him out of control!

(The only symptom Merle ever displayed to me of his possible alcohol problem was a broken leg he suffered shortly after I began studying with him. He wore it in a cast, which stayed with him, off and on, for the rest of his life. He told me that he'd been jumped by two drunks in a bar one night; one of them held him, while the second propped up his leg between two chairs, and then broke it frequently with a bat. Needless to say the leg never healed and it finally killed him, the leg, not the alcohol, but I don't really think it matters which to Merle.)

Merle and I had an understanding.

This was the deal: Merle could beat the living hell out of me (not literally, but figuratively), and I was free to quit if I didn't like it!

And he exercised his part of the bargain almost every week!

He was the most difficult man I have ever known in my life.

He wouldn't allow me to get away with anything.

If I let up a little on my practicing, he knew it.

If I played something sloppily, or carelessly, or thoughtlessly, he called me on it, every single time, and made me play it over and over and over again, until I got it just right.

Understand, to Merle, "just right" meant perfect, absolutely right.

And it didn't matter to Merle if the entire hour was taken up with one simple phrase; that's what we'd do, that one phrase, over and over and over again, until it fairly flew from my fingers on its own.

To get to Merle's, I'd take a bus from Anaheim to downtown Los Angeles, and then transfer to a second bus which would take me to

North Hollywood, where Merle's studio was. It was a long trip, up and back. At least three hours of bus riding for every hour of saxophone lesson.

But it didn't matter to Merle how many buses I took, or how far I had to come to study with him, or how young I was, or, for that matter, how big a pain in the ass he could be as a teacher.

Nothing mattered to Merle but the bargain we had struck, that it was his lot in life to teach people to become great saxophone players, and that people studied with him for exactly that reason.

And to Merle, anything I did, or failed to do, which violated that bargain, was grounds for immediate, and drastic, action.

On one occasion, only two minutes into the lesson, Merle cooly told me to pack up my saxophone and go back home. The lesson was over.

When I asked him why, he looked at me in disgust, and said, "Go."

I never did find out why he asked me to go home that particular day, but deep down in my heart I knew why.

It was because Merle knew I wasn't working as hard as I could.

Merle knew that I had a lazy streak in me a mile wide.

And I knew it too!

He wasn't only telling me to go home early, he was telling me to look at myself, to put myself into question.

To ask myself whether or not I was really serious about becoming a great saxophone player. Was I taking myself as seriously as Merle was?

Was I keeping my part of the bargain?

* * * *

I honestly can't tell you what kept me going back to get beat up by Merle week after week, month after month, year after year.

But I think it was the sound of my saxophone, as it changed, and grew, and matured, as it became music. Its depth, its range, its richness, its dexterity, its power all mesmerized me!

I remember how I would stand, sometimes for hours, in the bathroom at home with the door locked behind me and play the saxophone against the tiles in the shower.

How taken by surprise I would sometimes be by the rich, fat sound as it ricocheted off the tiles and the walls and out of the window, filling me with the most extraordinary feeling of wonder, of connection with myself and the world. How *old* that sound seemed to be—how alive!

Without Merle it wouldn't have happened.

* * * *

People who work in great companies—Power Point companies—think about them in exactly the same way as I think about Merle. It's a love-hate relationship.

An acquaintance of mine who graduated from West Point, earned an M.B.A. from Wharton, and then, as though that weren't enough, completed his sales apprenticeship at I.B.M., told me that nothing he had ever done in his life measured up to his I.B.M. experience.

"It was the toughest thing I had ever done," he told me, proudly.

"Without a doubt," he said, "No one, nothing, has ever tested me as completely as I.B.M. I loved that place."

And a friend of mine who worked intimately with Walt Disney, said of him, respectfully, "He was a monster. No one was tougher than Walt. No one expected more of you than Walt. No one rode you as hard, squeezed out the very last juice, kept digging until he found that very last nugget. Once he got it in his mind what he wanted to do, Walt wouldn't let anyone rest until they had done it."

They say the same about Ray Kroc, and Ross Perot, and Fred Smith, and the companies they created.

They loved the man and they hated him, they loved the company and they hated it.

So it seems that Power Point companies—indeed, all companies— take on the personalities of the people who create them.

And that is why so few companies have been successful in their attempt to develop managers into what have become labeled as *intrepreneurs.*

It's because personalities like Tom Watson's, Walt Disney's, Ray Kroc's, Ross Perot's, are so uncontrollable.

They are a force all their own, driven from within, unmanageable, chaotic, solitary, insatiable—possessed, you might say—exactly the opposite of what it takes to be a good manager.

You don't find people like them working in other people's companies for long.

That is why the companies they create—Power Point companies— demand more of their people than other companies do, because personalities like theirs demand more of *themselves* than other people do.

If my saxophone teacher, Merle, had, by an accident of fate, taken up business instead of the saxophone as his calling, I'm certain his company would have mirrored the ones I've just mentioned.

And that is because Merle expected more of himself and more of his students, than anyone has a right to expect in the ordinary world.

In the ordinary world, few people have the right to expect to become great saxophone players.

In Merle's world, nothing less would do.

In the ordinary world, few people have the right to create an amusement park as astonishingly unique as Disneyland is.

In Walt Disney's world, nothing less would do.

In the ordinary world, few people have the right to expect to create a chain of over 11,000 restaurants, all operating in an identical fashion, against the same rigorous standards.

In Ray Kroc's world, nothing less would do.

And so their companies often appear rigid from the outside.

And that's because they live by rules.

Walt's rules, or Ray's rules, or Tom's rules.

Tough rules, rules for a tough world, where ordinary people are unaccustomed to playing.

But, despite outward appearances—despite the seeming rigidity of their rules—the truly difficult characteristic of Power Point companies for ordinary people to take, isn't that they play by tough rules, *but that they are avid breakers of the very rules they make.*

The rules are constantly changing.

Power Point companies are continually rewriting their own traditions.

They are continually creating a new game to play.

And that is because the creators of Power Point companies are continually asking questions about how to get better; they are continually rising to their own expectations; they march to the beat of a different drummer. Marching to their own inner tune and living to a measure which comes from just around the corner, out of reach, out of sight, they are continually in a state of breaking up and reforming, and they do this as a matter of being, as a way of life; they couldn't do it any other way.

But their energy, their creativity, their spirit, their drive, their stamina—as essential as these traits are—aren't enough.

If they were, there would be many more Power Point companies than there are.

No, it seems also that the creators of Power Point companies possess, to a degree which puts the rest of us to shame, the five essential skills I spoke about earlier.

They concentrate, discriminate, organize, innovate, and communicate in such a way that puts focus, tension, order—a presence—at the heart of the enterprise which causes it to almost shimmer with ecstasy as it goes its unusual way.

It is that *shimmer,* that brightness, that radiance—are these words too strong?—that almost instantly distinguishes a Power Point company from all the others, from the inside and from the outside—in the hearts of those people with whom it comes into contact.

It is that the game is more important to such companies than the reward, which excites people so much.

But, that *still* is not enough.

There is something else about a Power Point company which endows it with such a tangible difference.

And it is that these businesses, these Power Point companies are created, not by business people, not by so-called entrepreneurs, as is commonly thought, but—and there is no other way to say it—by *children!*

These Power Point companies are created by the youngest part of us, not the most adult.

They are created by that part of us which believes it has the right to expect the world to change, to give us everything we want, exactly as we imagine it.

Not the methodical part, the dependable part, the reliable part, the responsible part, the grown up in us all, the part one expects the manager to play.

Not the adult who has learned to limit his or her expectations, but the child who wants it all.

I think of John Anderson and I immediately know that it was the *child* in him who created that 1947 Ford coupe.

I think of Marty Weissberg and I immediately know that it was the *child* in him who created that store.

I think of Merle, and I immediately know that it was the *child* in him who expected so much to come from my horn.

At times, I remember, he would stand beside me with obvious impatience as I was playing my horn, and actually stamp his feet, that's right, jump up and down, as if by stamping his feet he could force the sound out of my horn which I was incapable of forcing out myself!

He so much wanted to hear that sound!

Who does that but a child?

No wonder there are so few Power Point companies around.

It's because business, as it is ordinarily played, is so unattractive to most children.

It is such a dead and empty game.

❋ ❋ ❋ ❋

Let me tell you the story of another great business—a Power Point company in the making.

Let me give you a profound example of how the emotional preferences of people have been so well served, and how this quality alone has enabled one small business to thrive under conditions which would put most businesses under.

Let me tell you a story about a woman named Mary, and a vocational school in the field of massage therapy called The Holistic Health Institute.

❋ ❋ ❋ ❋

Settling down to Mary Conner Brown was a color of a different kind.

Putting it mildly, she had led a traveler's life.

From the moment Mary graduated from the University of North Carolina in 1972, with a B.S. in Psychology, she hit the road, and for the next five years she rarely stopped in any one place for more than a minute and a half.

As Mary puts it, she wasn't really looking for anything in particular, she was just restless.

She had this burning desire to *do* something, to make some kind of a mark on the world, to create an impact which would cause people to say, "Mary was here." It took on a physical form, starting, you might say, with her feet—they just wouldn't stop.

Shortly after graduating, Mary heard about, sought out, and immediately joined a commune in Virginia called Twin Trees, which was built on the principles of Skinner's *Walden Two.* There Mary alternately worked on the construction team as a plumber, the kitchen team as a cook, and the child care team as a surrogate mother.

Mary remembers the commune as "a powerfully transformational experience."

"It was a true matriarchy, created by women, for women, a place where, for the first time in my life, it became abundantly clear to me that I could damn well do anything I wanted to do.

"Here I was working as a plumber, for God's sake, when just a few months before I couldn't have told you the difference between a pipe wrench and a hammer!

"At Twin Trees, my restlessness—what I thought of at the time as my Search—became focused less on the question of what to do with my life, than on what do I *want* to do with my life?

"The realization that there was a huge difference between those two questions opened up a whole new world to me."

It wasn't long, however, before Mary discovered that, despite its lofty ambitions, Twin Trees had become its own sort of prison, a place so charismatic, so seductive, yet so oppressive, that she knew she had better get out.

As Mary tells it, "It was incredible for me to discover how powerful a hold the commune had on me. The very thing that empowered me there, began to control me. It was like a narcotic. Something in me told me that if I stayed much longer, I would find it difficult, if not impossible, to leave.

"The very next day I literally escaped in a visitor's car by hiding on the floor behind the driver's seat! The guy was shocked to find me there, but agreed to drop me off sixty miles away in Virginia Beach. Why I chose Virginia Beach is still a mystery to me, I think it was the only place that came to mind. It amazes me to this day. In only a couple of hours my entire life had completely changed! Here I was, at 3 o'clock on a Thursday afternoon, in a strange town, with no identity, no job, no place to live, only $18 to my name, and absolutely no idea of what I was going to do next. I loved it, and I was scared shitless! It was like waking up on a strange planet."

That very afternoon Mary rented a $15 a week room in a Boarding Hotel, and, with only $3 left to her name, began hustling "survival money" doing odd jobs on the streets of Virginia Beach, wondering what the next step in her odyssey would be.

The street became another first for Mary.

Her resilience and resourcefulness were tested over and over again.

Unlike home, college, and the commune, there were no rules on the street, no ritual to which Mary had to conform. No one told her what she had to do, or that she had to do anything.

She made it up as she went along, creating her own rules, her own aims.

Every day became a new opportunity, a new problem.

If she was good—or lucky—she got work; if she wasn't, she didn't.

A fast student, she quickly learned the difference between the two.

It quickly became a practice.

It gave her something of value to teach.

She was developing her style.

❊   ❊   ❊   ❊

A company is only as alive as its people.

The vitality of the product of a company, what it sells—its "commodity"—always reflects the emotional vitality of its people.

Put more directly, dumb commodities are created by dumb people.

I think it is also true that commodities mature—become dumber—not *only* as they outwear their usefulness—for example, their perceived value to their customer—but as the vitality of the people who create them wanes, disintegrates, becomes less intense, less joyful.

On the other hand, the emotional vitality of a company's people is *always* a function of the emotional vitality of the founder, or CEO, of that company.

An old Sicilian expression, "the fish stinks from the head down," tells us where one should look for the failure of a company to thrive.

It's a reliable axiom that dead CEOs create dead companies.

CEOs who are satisfied with themselves create self-satisfied companies.

Dull CEOs create dull companies.

Belligerent CEOs create belligerent companies.

Adventurous CEOs create adventurous companies.

Fearful CEOs create fearful companies.

What goes around comes around.

Most companies fail because there is something missing—some key and critical component left out.

The CEO is adventurous, but lazy, so the details don't get worked out.

The CEO is passionate, but stupid, so there is force, but in the wrong direction.

The CEO is dissatisfied with him or herself, but places blame on his or her people instead, so "the search" turns into a witch hunt.

Or the CEO is a genius, but crazy, and so the energy of his or her genius is transformed into a stew pot of confusion.

There is no escaping it; if you want to understand Frank Lorenzo, look at Eastern Airlines.

What's missing in his company is what's missing in him.

This game we call business is a delicate, delicate thing.

※　※　※　※

For the next four years, Mary Brown stumbled from one adventure to another, moved more by instinct than anything else.

A stranger on the street got her a job in a beer bar, "slinging suds."

A chance encounter in the bar turned into a roommate and a relationship aboard a 35-foot sailboat aptly named *Chance Encounter,* in which she and her new friend sailed to the Bahamas, the Virgin Islands, the Florida Keys, and the Tortugas, working as they went, diving for conch, chartering out, or whatever showed up.

As Mary describes it, "Whatever happened, happened. Something in me craved experience—new impressions. Somehow I knew that the only way I would grow was if I let go of my past and walked willingly into an unknown, an unforeseeable, an uncontrollable future. What's most true of that time in my life is that I simply allowed events to shape me. I was smart enough to know that I didn't know enough to shape events. It's not that I was fearless, as a lot of people think when I tell them about those times, but that I simply made room for my fear to exist without allowing it to control me. You might say that my fear and I established a working relationship with each other."

It was during that freewheeling time that Mary's school was born.

✻ ✻ ✻ ✻

Who can say why things happen?

Who can say where anything begins?

But it's instructive to try.

It's of value to look for origins, beginnings, where things begin to go off or on track.

For it is undeniable that every single thing, every event, every condition, has its beginning—was started, or was born, or was ignited—at some single point in time. Whether or not we know when, where, or why, it did happen, it did start, it did come together.

But the most instructive origins are not in the past; they are happening right now.

New things, new ventures, new companies—new *lives*—are continuously beginning. At this very instant—in this micro-second, in this flash of contracted time—something new is setting its foot down on a totally new path, is suddenly decided, is charting its course, is creating a future of what will also become past and present events—each existing on the very edge of future instants, future beginnings, and future endings.

It is in the miracle of *occurrence*—this living moment—that everything begins, that everything ends, even businesses, as they have begun, and ended, for all time.

＊　＊　＊　＊

So I think that Tom Peters was wrong.

It's not the *pursuit* of excellence that matters.

It's that we are pursued *by* excellence.

It's that the question of excellence resides as a possibility in everything we do.

It's not that the gas station is clean that's important, it's that somebody was possessed by the need to clean it.

It's the fire at the heart of life itself, this excellence, that either possesses us, or not.

And it is in this instant that it happens, not in the past, not in the future, but at the very instant of choice, now, in this very instant, as our businesses, as our very lives, are being shaped.

What concerns me, what should concern us all I think, is how few of us seem to be available—or willing—to be possessed.

＊　＊　＊　＊

It is astonishing to think that Mary's business was started with a book about massage and a handful of clients, both of which (the book and the clients) were given to Mary by a massage therapy friend who decided to leave town.

Mary read the book and massaged the clients, and thus her school was born.

How Mary Brown came upon the idea for her school isn't important, you couldn't replicate it even if you wanted to.

The simple matter is that she was passionately seeking something and she found it.

Don't misunderstand me, it wasn't the school she was seeking—the business never is, not for Disney, not for Kroc, not for Smith, not for Perot, not for Mary. No, the school—the business—is simply the medium through which such people hope to find what they're looking for.

For Mary Brown, the school was, and still is, a mirror—a reflection of her true self.

She sees herself in it every single day.

It is a product of who she is.

It is a continuing commentary on what she has learned, and on what she hasn't.

It is—like the streets of Virginia Beach—a difficult place to go to sleep.

❋   ❋   ❋   ❋

In August 1990, Mary, like all the other owners of vocational schools with student aid programs in her state, was peremptorily notified by the state that the rules for such vocational schools were about to be changed.

"Changed," however, is too mild a word for what the state had in mind.

What the state had in mind was a revolution.

And this revolution was going to take place immediately.

And anyone who didn't comply immediately with the state's new rules, would be found in violation, and could be put out of business.

What the state decided to do was to make it very difficult for a vocational school offering student aid programs to stay in business.

The state had decided to create a new game, a game called, "Try this one on for size."

Just a few examples:

What the state said was that such schools could no longer pay their sales staff commissions for enrollments until the students they enrolled graduated from school, forcing schools to create a totally new compensation system for their sales people (at great additional expense to the school), and take the risk of losing all their sales staff at the same time.

The state didn't care.

What the state said was that any student on financial aid had the right to drop out of school at any time and receive a full pro rata refund of their unearned tuition, forcing schools to rethink their entire financial strategy, their capital requirements, their financial aid programs—without any data to support their conclusions.

The state didn't care.

What the state said was that the school had to guarantee that at least 70 percent of its graduating students would be fully employed in the field for which they were trained within six months of graduating, or the school would be in default.

Can you imagine what would happen to state universities and colleges if the same rules applied to them? That all psychology students who had received financial aid had to be employed as psychologists within six months of graduation; that all music students who had received financial aid had to be employed as musicians within six months of graduation; that all teaching students who had received financial aid had to be employed as teachers within six months of graduation; and that all engineering students who had received financial aid had to be employed as engineers within six months of graduation?

Do you suppose state schools could survive under those rules?

Could your business?

What if the state required you to guarantee your product or service?

What if the state demanded that you provide your people with a guarantee of success when you hire them?

What if the state told you how much capital your business needed to have in relationship to your revenue in order for you to be permitted to stay in business?

What your net profit needed to be in order for you to be permitted to stay in business?

What you could say, and what you couldn't say to your customer in your marketing process in order for you to be permitted to stay in business?

Well, the state said these things, and much more to the vocational schools doing business there.

But, what the state didn't say was how it came to these brilliant conclusions.

Instead, what the state did was to shove dozens of small vocational schools to the very brink of financial disaster, and put many others out of business.

As you might imagine, most of the schools, small and large, were simply unprepared, and therefore unable to comply.

But, on September 1, 1990, when all schools were expected to be in compliance, *with only two weeks notice*, Mary's school had fulfilled every single requirement imposed on it.

She had done the impossible in record time.

✳   ✳   ✳   ✳

Mary was able to accomplish the impossible in record time because her school possesses something few businesses possess.

The people who work for her, buy from her, sell to her, and loan her money, love her and the school she has created.

They think she's incredible.

And, the simple truth of it is, they're right.

Mary has created a wonder out of nothing.

Her school was started in a small, shabby house with six students, no capital, and absolutely no business experience of any kind.

But, she knew about people, and what it took to survive on the streets.

More importantly, she knew that she wanted to teach her students more than a skill.

She wanted to teach them what she had learned, and she wanted to teach them what she hadn't.

She wanted to teach people that it was possible to have work they love, and to have it on their own terms.

But she also wanted to teach people what it takes to make it on their own—to become independent of the system, to grow, and expand, and thrive, as she had, to take risks, as she had, to test themselves, as she had—without any certainty, or any guarantee whatsoever that the end would justify the means.

Mary was afire with her convictions, and absolutely inspired by what she was about to do!

And what she was about to do was learn.

❊ ❊ ❊ ❊

There are seven rules Mary learned about building an emotionally vital business.

The first rule Mary learned is that people need order. They need to know that there is a structure, a logic, a foundation, a clear set of standards, of principles, a fairness about the business and the job they are there to do.

The second rule Mary learned is that people need to feel heard. They need to know that their contribution is important, that no matter where they stand in relationship to the business—as employee, as customer, as supplier, as lender—what they want matters, and that there is a channel through which they can express what matters to them, and that the channel is always open.

The third rule Mary learned is that people need to feel connected to something bigger than they are. If the business has small aims, is simply interested in surviving, in staying in business, it will not sustain them, it will not touch them, it will not engage them. No, the business has to take on something—*no matter what kind of a business it is*—in an important way. It has to be willing to tilt at windmills, the bigger the better. People are dying for want of something larger than life to believe in, to rally around, to support.

The fourth rule Mary learned is that people need to have a purpose. They need to have a plan. They need to be going someplace—some place specific, in a specific amount of time. Without a purpose people begin to wallow, to become suspended in time. They become a drag on each other, begin to feel victimized, lose track of the time, go to movies and forget what they've seen.

The fifth rule Mary learned is that people need to feel that what they are doing has moral weight. The business has to be concerned about what is right. What is right for themselves, what is right for others, and what is right for the world. The business has to operate with *conscience*. Without conscience, a business is a drag on what little self-esteem people already possess.

The sixth rule Mary learned is that people need to feel that what they personally do is important. They need to feel that the business, without them, somehow wouldn't matter as much. That when they walk in the door, something vital is added to the business—something only they can bring to the table. They need to feel that if they were no longer there the business wouldn't be the same.

And finally, the seventh rule Mary learned about the emotional health of a business is that people need to feel that the people they associate with love them.

That, no matter what, people care.

A student of Mary Brown's wrote:

> *Mary C. Brown, what a lady!*
> *She beats my brain out daily.*
> *She's rough, she's tough,*
> *But she knows her stuff.*
> *(And she can charm the socks off a baby!)*

I love you, Mary C. Brown.

6.
THE THIRD CATEGORY OF PREFERENCE: THE FUNCTIONAL IDEAL

I've noticed that people who have never worked with steel have trouble seeing this . . . that the motorcycle is primarily a mental phenomenon.

—*Robert M. Pirsig,*
Zen and the Art of Motorcycle Maintenance

That a company *looks* great and *feels* great is still insufficient for a company to *act* great.

For a company to act great requires it to think in a significantly different way about what it does and how it does it than most companies are prepared to do.

That is because most companies are *people-oriented,* rather than *process-oriented.*

People-oriented companies focus their attention on *who* is doing the work.

Process-oriented companies focus their attention on whether the right work is being done, and more importantly, if the right work is being done, how is it being done.

People-oriented companies depend upon "good" people to produce results, where "good" is defined as experienced, successful, self-motivated—in short, people who can be depended upon to produce good results. Someone is always shouting "Find me someone who knows how to get the job done!" in a people-oriented company.

On the other hand, process-oriented companies depend upon good *processes* to produce results, where good is defined as the process's ability to produce the very best results in the hands of inexperienced (or less experienced) people than the competition needs to produce the same results.

It's valuable to note that most of the people-oriented companies I have known (and I have known thousands of them) are almost always intolerably self righteous about their great people orientation, ("We're a *people* company!"), when in fact they are usually far less people-oriented than they would have us believe.

When something goes wrong in a people-oriented business someone invariably asks the question, "What's wrong with Jack?"

(It's a sine qua non that in people-oriented companies somebody's always letting the company down. If the definition of good people is people who produce good results, logic would tell us that when people fail to produce good results, they're not good people. Not a cheery position to be in.)

On the other hand, when something goes wrong in a true process-oriented company, the question that invariably is asked first is "What's wrong with the *process?*"

("Jack" isn't the problem, the process is.)

One might argue, "Ah, yes, but who creates the process in the first place but 'good' people?"

And I would respond, "People using a process!"

❊   ❊   ❊   ❊

A people-oriented company's strategy is almost always different than a process-oriented company's strategy.

A people-oriented company first looks for the best person for the job—somebody who already knows how to do it, has done it very successfully in the past, and is self-motivated to do it.

Should such a person be found, the people-oriented company will most often provide the new person with an "orientation," a generalized review of housekeeping principles—"This is where you get the grease; this is where we keep the pencils; this is where you can buy some coffee; this is Fred; this is Jocko; this is Myrtle"—and then leave the new person to get on with what they hired him or her to do, to find his or her own way, to do the job the best way he or she can.

Failing to find the best person, a people-oriented company will resort to teaching as "good" a person as it can find the skills needed to perform effectively on the job, and then show him or her where the grease is, where the pencils are, where he or she can buy some coffee, this is Fred, this is Jocko, this is Myrtle, and finally give the new person "the room" to decide how he or she prefers to do the job.

(Skills must be differentiated here from process, in that skills as they are commonly taught in people-oriented companies are those basic skills used by all companies of the same category—for example, all auto repair shops, or all poodle clipping shops, or all insurance companies—to get the job done in an undifferentiated way. Process-oriented companies, however, design processes which are unique to that company so as to get the job done in a way that preferentially differentiates that company from its competitors—faster, smoother, less expensive, with a unique flourish.)

A process-oriented company knows that the discovery of a better way to do something is significantly more empowering than finding a better person to do it.

A process-oriented company knows that you can always lose the better person (indeed, in this day and age you always do!), but that it's much more difficult to lose a better process. (People aren't the exclusive property of your company but your processes can be.)

In short, process-oriented companies know that a better process can be liberating in that it has the power of turning ordinary people into extraordinary people. (The best people can be a limiting factor in that there are so few of them that you have to pay a premium to get them. Once you do get them, they can hold you at ransom if they decide they're bored with the present arrangement. Or if it's just not quite right today. Or if they need a vacation you hadn't planned for. Or for any reason—of theirs—at all! Then try to *replace* them!)

※   ※   ※   ※

Now I know that if you're what would be categorized on the job as a "best person" this whole concept may offend you, and I apologize for the offense, but the good news is that a great process in the hands of a great person is a wonder to behold!

Witness *Hamlet* and Laurence Olivier.

Witness Beethoven's Fifth Symphony and Leonard Bernstein.

Witness Joe Montana and a football.

Witness a star at anything, and you'll understand what I mean.

Every great person uses a great process.

The question here is, who owns the process?

※   ※   ※   ※

For a process to be liberating it must liberate everyone—the employee, the customer, the supplier, and the lender.

Such process-oriented companies as Supercuts, Lenscrafters, Midas Mufflers, Instant Lube, Merry Maid, Mrs. Field's Cookies, Pizza

Hut, Subway Sandwiches—and of course, McDonald's, Disneyland, and Federal Express—and many, many more, all produce liberating results for their employees, their customers, their suppliers, and their lenders.

The process assures all of them a measure of predictability that few businesses produce for *anyone,* let alone for all four.

Supercuts possesses a process for cutting hair which enables a beginner to produce a professional result in short order at half the price a professional must charge.

Lenscrafters possesses a process for creating quality eyeglasses "in about an hour" for people who simply can't, or don't want to, wait any longer.

Merry Maid possesses a process for cleaning a house, efficiently, effectively, exactly as you want it, by personnel who are clean, dependable, and productive.

All differentiate themselves not by the people who work for them, but by the process through which these people produce a predictable result each and every time.

And because they possess a *process* that works, their *people* are perceived to work better than most.

※　※　※　※

Think about it this way, there is a way to do everything.

And if that is true, then there must be a better way to do everything.

And if that is true, then there must be a *best way* to do everything.

Not the *only* way, mind you, not absolutely and forever the best way. But the relatively best way, the way that produces the best results as perceived by the people with whom it interacts, the way that performs best in relationship to all the other options available at this time and for the foreseeable future.

That is what process-oriented companies are all about, discovering the *best way.*

But, where they start is not with *how* to do it, but with the question, "What is the best thing to do?"

And the question, "What is the best thing to do?" can only be answered by understanding what people want most.

※   ※   ※   ※

A *best way* process is discovered by answering the following questions:

1. What one thing would our customers, employees, suppliers, and lenders most like us to do for them that we and our competitors can't currently do?
2. Has anyone ever tried to do this thing?
3. If yes, why did they fail?
4. What would it mean to us if we could do it?
5. Why can't we do it?
6. What would be the *best way* to do it?
7. How much would it cost us to be able to do it the *best way?*
8. Is it worth the cost?
9. If yes, what would be the impact on our customers, employees, suppliers, lenders?
10. If negative for any or all, how would we overcome that negative?
11. If we can't overcome the negative, do the benefits outweigh the negative aspects?
12. If we can, should we do it?

※   ※   ※   ※

The *best way* is always the way which eliminates the Primary Frustration experienced by any one of the four Primary Influencers of a business.

What is the Primary Frustration?

Just what you might think.

The Primary Frustration is the negative experience most commonly complained about concerning someone's interaction with a business.

It's not difficult to find out what the Primary Frustration is.

For example, ask 100 people who have done business with a building contractor about the transaction, and at least 75 will say, "The job wasn't completed when they said it would be; there was always an excuse."

Ask 100 people who have had their auto repaired about the transaction, and at least 80 will say, "I felt totally out of control, and they made me feel worse."

Ask 100 people who have been to a doctor about the transaction, and at least 90 will say, "I waited!"

Stereotypes? True. But, it is in these stereotypical responses that one finds the Primary Frustration and the *best way.*

What would happen to the general contractor who says, "At Heartfelt Construction we are always on time, on price, and deliver a spotless performance—or we pay for it, Guaranteed!"

What would happen to the auto repair shop that says, "When something goes wrong with your car, the one thing you *don't* need is more worry. At Hearthstone Auto, you'll *always* have a good experience—or the job's on us. Guaranteed!"

What would happen to the medical office that says, "At Sweet Water Medical Office, we *always* keep our appointments on time—or we pay for the visit. Guaranteed!"

What would happen if they actually did these things?

If they actually pulled them off?

If they eliminated, once and for all, the Primary Frustration normally experienced by most people who interact with their kinds of businesses day after day?

If they were to set their attention on it until their business became a master at performing the impossible?

Wouldn't that make a difference to the people who buy from them, the people who work for them, the people who sell to them, and the people who lend to them?

Wouldn't that have a positive impact on everyone involved?

Wouldn't that set their business apart?

Isn't that obvious?

Well, that's what process-oriented companies are all about.

Inventing an *un*obvious way to do the obvious, every single time.

※　※　※　※

To make a promise—and to accept full responsibility for the delivery of that promise—requires control. The kind of control that only a process-oriented company can hope to exercise.

Let me tell you about just such a company, Santos Construction. A small business that determined what the Primary Frustration of their customer was, and decided to do something bold about it.

❋ ❋ ❋ ❋

Marino Santos used to wear black to work every day, except for a bright red scarf he wore as a sweatband which also served to tie back his crow-black hair.

Marino Santos loved the color black.

To him, black signified mastery, singleness of purpose, seriousness, and also danger.

Black was the color by which Marino Santos marked the barriers which distinguished him, and therefore separated him, from the rest of the world. Black warned the world that Marino Santos was a serious fellow, not to be fooled with.

Black was his shield.

On the other hand, red was the color of Marino Santos' heart.

His bright red scarf signified to Marino Santos the passion of his interest. It was the hot, restless flame at the center of his life, the intense fire which burned inside of him, inside the black container, the cold shield of his distance.

While his black clothes said, "I stand alone," his red scarf said, "I'm about to explode!"

And explode he did, every day at work. It was in the nature of the work that he did.

Marino Santos was what is called in the construction trade, a framer. He and his small crew subcontracted the framing of homes in Southern California, Arizona, Nevada, Colorado, wherever the work was.

To the general contractors who hired them, they were simply known as Santo's crew. Inside the small company, however—more like a small band of men than an actual business—they thought of themselves as *"Los apasionados sin igual"*—"the only ones".

Everyone in the trade knew Santos' crew. Among their peers, Marino Santos and his band were the stuff of folklore. It was not only that they were the best at what they did—and there was no doubt in anyone's mind that they were—but there was the mystique, the *machismo,* which accompanied them everywhere they went.

Like the stars they were, Santos' crew remained aloof. At breaks, they would gather together, seated in a small tight circle on a concrete slab facing each other while they quietly drank their coffee, ate their burritos, and whispered among themselves—star talk, no one knew about what.

But when Marino Santos and his crew went to work, there was nothing quiet about them at all. Their framing hammers fairly flew! Walls went up in record time—first one house, and then another, emerging as though miraculously from the concrete slabs. You could literally watch them grow, they went so fast—with Marino Santos in the middle of it all, his long, muscular arm with its shining bluesteel hammer, as if growing out of his hand, wailing away at the wood, *thwack, thwack, thwack,* his strong melodic voice singing among them, calling out names, swearing at the sky. And they did it to music! For Marino Santos' crew, every day on the job was a performance, a dance, a physical and visual crusade. *"Los apasionados sin igual"*—"the only ones". It was what they did. It was their signature. It was what they were known for. It was what they lived to do. It was who they were.

And then, early one Wednesday morning in the middle of July, on the way to a job in Barstow, Marino Santos' pickup blew a tire and flew off the road at 90 miles an hour and turned over five times until it finally came to rest upside down against a boulder.

For thirteen hours Marino Santos lay trapped in his truck with a broken back before he was finally discovered by the Highway Patrol.

That he survived the accident was a miracle.

But he was out of the framing business for good.

❊   ❊   ❊   ❊

What does a framer do when he can't frame anymore?

Especially when he's a man like Marino Santos?

What does a star do when the very thing at which he excels is suddenly taken away from him?

What does a man who uses his body for a living do when his body can no longer perform?

What does a company do when it has built its ability to perform on the skills of a handful of good people and they're suddenly gone?

❊   ❊   ❊   ❊

For the first six months or so, Marino Santos did little or nothing but drink. He woke up in the morning and drank. And he didn't stop until he passed out at night.

At times he would get so furious with his condition that he would heave an empty whiskey bottle through the closed bedroom window and into the street and sit there in his wheelchair amid the shards of broken glass screaming into the night at anyone who would listen. The police would come by, but they wouldn't do anything other than threaten to take him in.

His crew came to visit him every day. They hated to see him like he was. They called him names. They cried with him. They sat silently by and said nothing. They threatened that they wouldn't come back anymore. They played music and drank with him. They did whatever they could for both him and themselves—sometimes just to be there was enough.

And then, as suddenly as it began, it was over.

One day he seemed just as bad, and the next day he was better.

He called his crew together.

"I want to apologize to all of you," he said.

"Not for the past six months, not for the drinking—I couldn't help that.

"I want to apologize for the framing, for the arrogance, for the belief I had in my body, for being so stupid.

"I don't want to be stupid anymore." Marino Santos said.

"It's time to start a new business."

※　※　※　※

Marino Santos didn't care what his new business was, although he knew it would have something to do with construction. Construction was in his blood. He loved the smell of raw wood. He loved seeing things start from nothing and become something almost overnight. He loved the physical impact it had on the world. It was a mark of his having been there. It was something you could touch and look at for years after.

Yes, it had to be construction, but other than that it didn't matter what kind of construction it was.

Except for this: The construction his new business did was going to have as profound an impact on the people around him as his old business did, except that the new business would not depend upon his, or his crew's, physical skills. The business would work without them.

At first his men didn't understand. They had always worked with their bodies. They had always taken pride in their extraordinary physical skill. Not to work like that anymore didn't make sense. Their joy was to express themselves physically, to move on the concrete slab, to raise walls, to walk the rafters. To think of not doing these things any more created great sadness in all of them.

But, because they cared for and respected Marino Santos so much, they listened. And gradually, it came to them that what Marino Santos was talking about wouldn't deprive them of anything, but would give them something they had never had.

In one of their many conversations together, Marino Santos said, "I have thought about this a good deal. It comes down to this. Either we work for a living, like *burros,* until we can't work any more—" he spread his arms as if to say, I am the proof, "or we find a way to build a business that works for us. We *think* about this business, we put our minds to it, we shape it so that it works like we have learned to work, with precision, with joy, with energy. But we must find a way to do this without people like us. People like us who take pride in being separate from the world, people like us who need to be alone, people like us will eventually kill our business, as I have almost killed our business. No, we must build a business that can make it easy for people who are not like us, and who will never be like us, to act like us. It is our fierce pride which makes us so good. We must learn how to give this fierce pride to people who do not possess it naturally. We must make it possible for everyone who works in our business to become as good as we are as long as they work in our business. That will be our gift to them. We must find a way to do this.

"Our business will give them something they can't get elsewhere in the world. And, as a result of that, they will stay, and our business will flourish. That will be their gift to us. Those who are like us, however, the other *los apasionados sin igual* in the world, must do what they must do. There is nothing we can do for them.

"As always, they are on their own. They would not have it any other way."

Marino Santos paused briefly, and looked seriously into his men's eyes, his black eyes shining.

"Brothers, what I wish for us to do will be a risky venture. I have no way of knowing if we will be successful or not. But I know in my heart it is the path for us to follow."

＊　＊　＊　＊

As always, once they made their minds up, Marino Santos and his crew took their new path seriously.

In accordance with Marino Santos' instructions, each man took it as his personal mission to find work in some segment of the construction industry which was new to him.

They segmented the industry into new construction and reconstruction, commercial and residential. They then broke each segment into parts, to find out which segment and which part of that segment was most promising as a business opportunity.

Marino Santos told them that time was not important. What was important was making certain of their ultimate selection—that it be the single segment of the construction industry which could provide them with the greatest opportunity to achieve their objective.

It had to be a segment of the industry which had a consistent growth pattern, did not experience sharp up and down swings because of the economy, was relatively compartmentalized—that is, repeated the same tasks much the same way from job to job—wasn't capital intensive to either start or maintain, and could be operated independently of other contractors—that is, could secure, start, and complete a contract without having to depend upon subcontractors or general contractors to do their parts of the job.

Marino Santos' kitchen served as their operations center.

Every night after work, the men reported their findings over a cold beer.

There were heated arguments. Each man came to conclusions which others refuted. But gradually, as the men became smarter about their mission, more intelligent about their conclusions, and more eloquent in the positions each took, their arguments became less heated, though no less intense.

Marino Santos's strategy was simple: as one industry segment after another was excluded as an option, the men who were employed in those segments would leave them to find work in the remaining segments, until finally they would all be working in the same industry segment—the segment of choice—but for competing contractors.

And that's exactly what happened.

After two and a half years of dedicated work, research, and planning, Marino Santos and his men found themselves decided.

It was such a simple, uncomplicated decision when they finally came to it.

They would go into the kitchen remodeling business.

And they would call it Three Day Kitchens.

※　※　※　※

On the face of it, there is something so ordinary about business.

Something so unimportant, so trivial.

For Marino Santos and his men to apply themselves so determinedly, to expend so much effort and time to the ordinary task of deciding what business to go into, to spend all that energy merely to start a kitchen remodeling business, when instead they could have done . . . what?

What else would a man like Marino Santos do?

Join the Peace Corps?

Graduate from M.I.T.?

Enter a monastery?

Try out for the Olympics?

Write a book?

What better could any of us do than he?

How many people do you know who have expended as much effort, intelligence, care, or attention on the selection of a path?

How many people do you know who have taken such a passionate interest in every single thing they do?

How many people do you know who could remember their aim for as long as two and a half years with only their own interest to remind them of it, who could bring the energy and attention of a group of strong-willed people to bear down on a problem that had no end in sight, and still maintain that energy and attention as well as Marino Santos did, and who could keep that attention from wavering, from getting lost among the daily concerns which plague us all, and certainly must have plagued him?

Who do you know who possesses such force of purpose?

Such impeccable will?

What difference does it make what the business is after all?

Or that it is a business?

These men—these *apasionados sin igual*—could have been climbing the Himalayas and it wouldn't have added one thing to their journey.

❋ ❋ ❋ ❋

In fact, it was at least two more years before Marino Santos and his men completed their first kitchen for pay.

They installed hundreds of kitchens for practice.

Every conceivable problem was faced, agonized over, dealt with, and overcome.

They worked at night and on weekends in a warehouse Marino Santos rented, in which they constructed dozens of practice kitchen construction sites. Every kitchen problem his men faced during their day on the job was put on paper at night and analyzed, scrutinized, discussed, argued about, until every peculiarity, every exception, every unpredictable variable faced in the kitchen remodeling business had been reviewed at least a dozen times—and sometimes even more often than that, looking for the similiarities, the predictable, the standardizing opportunities.

No one, they were sure, had ever spent as much time, trouble, and intelligence to solve the problems associated with kitchen remodeling.

They were determined to get it right.

They were going to create a kitchen remodeling system such as the world had never seen, that could produce an absolutely predictable result in the hands of novice workmen trained only in their system, and they were going to figure out how to do it—how to completely renovate and remodel any kitchen—walls, windows, floors, cabinets, lighting, plumbing—all within no more than three days. Guaranteed!

And they were going to figure out how to do it at a cost significantly below the competition, at a quality significantly better than any one around, and at a profit which would justify it being done at all.

The competition, Marino Santos discovered (though he wasn't surprised), was not the problem.

There was no competition. Not for the company he intended to create.

His men reported daily on the waste, inefficiency, lack of skill, disinterest, and lack of management on the jobs they were working.

Materials and men rarely showed up on time, and sometimes never.

The job site was usually a mess.

"They are pigs," one of his men reported disdainfully.

Where heavy reconstruction was required and surprises were discovered (as they often were), the job could be delayed for hours, even days, until the almost always absent contractor, or his foreman if he had one, showed up to personally solve the problem.

No, as Marino Santos knew only so well, contractors were not fastidious men.

Shoddy work was normal, there was no training.

Experienced people were either hired out of the hall, off the street, or as subcontractors. The margins were so thin that there was no time, money, or people to spend on developing new people.

No, other contractors would not determine Three Day Kitchens' success or failure. He and his men would.

They worked like they had never worked before.

They were determined to get it right.

※　※　※　※

A kitchen, more than any other room in a house, is built to certain predictable standards.

Approached randomly, that is, without a data base of *quantified* experience, it might seem that every kitchen presents a unique problem—that every one is different. This is not the case.

Unfortunately, few small remodeling contractors have ever quantified any of their experience, and so what they find themselves dealing with day in and day out are seemingly uncommon, or problematic, conditions which always call for uncommon, and, usually, costly reactions.

Indeed, what Marino Santos and his crew discovered is that most of the kitchen work they monitored over the two years of their study, was predictably and monotonously the same, presenting measurably few variations on a repetitious theme.

Therefore, to invent a kitchen remodeling system which could guarantee an installed kitchen in exactly three days meant only that Marino Santos and his men had to determine what those variations on the theme were, create a variety of preplanned kitchen solutions to address each and every one of them, create a pre-programmed construction and installation strategy for each kitchen solution, recruit, hire, and then rigorously train a small crew of inexperienced technicians in their construction and installation system, and create a management system which would assure Marino Santos and his men that their system would be used exactly as planned, each and every time.

And then, practice, practice, practice these processes, over and over and over again, until there wasn't a question in anyone's mind that they could be implemented faithfully and impeccably every single time.

Marino Santos and his men boiled their mission down to five essential ingredients:

1. Control what is sold.
2. Control how it is sold.
3. Control how it is planned.
4. Control how it is built and installed.
5. Control how it is monitored.

The failure of a contractor to exercise control over any one of these Five Control Points, as Marino Santos and his men referred to them, meant that the job wouldn't be completed as promised.

That would not be a problem at Three Day Kitchens.

They renewed their intention each day.

※　※　※　※

The night following their first paid kitchen installation was a special night for Marino Santos and his men.

It had gone off without a hitch.

But they had known it would turn out that way long before the job began.

They had planned it that way, and they had practiced their process diligently. Nothing was taken for granted.

Their customer was astonished.

Not only was the job done exactly as promised, but the men who did it were astonishingly clean, well-organized, and fastidious in their comportment—"joyful," the customer said expressing her delight to Marino Santos about not only having the job done exactly as promised, but having experienced people who obviously loved their work so well.

"How do you find such good people?" she asked.

Marino Santos smiled, "I wish I knew." he said.

7.
THE FOURTH CATEGORY OF PREFERENCE: THE FINANCIAL IDEAL

Money, money, money. They're driving me crazy!
—Anonymous CEO

I'm going to change the tone right now.

I've got to tell you something truly important.

I want to talk about money.

Little did I know as I walked into my office at The Michael Thomas Corporation (MTC) on December 10, 1985, that neither my business nor my life would ever be the same again.

Nineteen eighty-five was a significant year for many reasons.

It was the year in which our business more than doubled in size, from $2 million in 1984, to $4.3 million in revenue.

Nineteen eighty-five was also the year in which we inaugurated our franchise program in earnest, by selling, training, and starting up 57 franchises throughout California whose purpose it was to deliver the proprietary small business service we had been developing at MTC since founding the company in 1977—a service we call The Michael Thomas Business Development Program.

In 1985, we were enrolling an average of 75 new small business clients in our program each month, in addition to the ongoing client base of 850 small businesses we served throughout California, and we had a dedicated, enthusiastic, and well-trained staff of over 100 people in client support services, program development, marketing, and finance, not including our franchisees and their employees.

In addition to everything else we accomplished in 1985, I also completed writing my first book, *The E-Myth.*

I had just married my wife Ilene, with whom I spent three wonderful weeks traveling in Paris and the south of France, after which we returned home to buy a large, elegant Spanish-style home in Hillsborough, California, just south of San Francisco.

In short, to me, my wife, and everyone else at MTC, 1985 was a year of unparalleled accomplishment, fulfillment, and promise.

Our company was an entrepreneurial dream come true.

My partner and I had started the company alone, with no money, a handful of clients, an office we couldn't afford, and the dream of creating a totally unique and affordable consulting service aimed at the millions of small mom-and-pop businesses in need of help the world over.

My wife, Ilene, joined us in 1982. Her extraordinary ability to develop people and systems pushed the company far beyond the place she found us; we took on a new life, a new vitality, a new focus, a sharper, clearer point of view.

Eight years after starting the company, and three years after Ilene joined us, everything we had planned for, worked for, and struggled for, was becoming a reality—was growing, just as we had hoped it would—before our very eyes.

Hundreds of clients attended our seminars every month.

Thousands of small businesses had participated in our program over the years.

Hundreds of thousands of small business employees were being positively impacted by the work we had done with the companies in which they were employed.

And this year, 1985, was the culmination of all of our work.

It was the most exhilarating year of my life!

Until that day when the dark, worried frown on my partner's face revealed to me that something else was going on—something I wasn't going to like.

※　※　※　※

As I look back over the five years which have transpired since the day I sat across from my partner and received the shock of my life, I have learned some things about money.

The most important thing I have learned is that we don't spend money as much as we consume it. Money is food.

We consume it and convert it into things—the feelings, associations, symbols, and statues we believe in.

That's what a consumer society really means.

It takes the material idea of money, ingests it, digests it, and converts it into its idea of living.

To some, money is converted into power.

To others, money is converted into security.

To others, money is converted into getting by the best way they can.

To others, money is converted into self-esteem.

To others, money is converted into survival.

To others, money is converted into scarcity.

To others, money is converted into magic.

To others, sex.

To still others, beauty.

To many, money is converted into sin.

And to still others, money is converted into evil.

The fact is that money does not exist without people.

Money has no meaning without people.

Money is simply an idea we have agreed upon.

An idea which represents to every one of us our net worth in the world.

※　※　※　※

I remember the exact words my partner said to me on the morning of December 10, 1985. I will never forget them.

He was sitting at his desk, his head hunched over his arms, his fingers pulling at his hair distractedly. He looked up at me briefly with a look that spelled disaster, and said in a voice I could hardly hear, "We blew it. We let it get away from us. I don't know what we were thinking about."

At first, I had difficulty understanding what he was telling me.

I thought that he was simply telling me that there was a problem we had to work out. Just another one of the many problems we had worked out together over the years. That would have been okay. We had solved problems before, in fact it was a way of life for us. We dealt with what we had to deal with; that's what our partnership had been all about—getting through the tough stuff, handling what had to be handled, solving the problems as they got in our way.

But, that wasn't what he was saying.

What he was really saying—what I finally fully grasped—was that, according to him, this wasn't simply another one of those problems. This time we had really done it. We were broke! The business was insolvent. We had *really* blown it, once and for all. As far as he was concerned, it was all over. He could see no way out.

I was stunned. It wasn't possible. How could it be? We had taken in more money this year than ever before. And, according to the financial information I had seen, we were operating at a healthy profit. Everything was working in the business according to plan— franchise sales exceeded expectations, cash flow was better than expected, training of franchisees was completed and on schedule. Not one word had been mentioned to me about financial problems brewing. I stood there stupidly, struck dumb with fear and self-loathing. I didn't know what to say, what to ask, other than, "How bad is it? What specifically is wrong?"

He didn't even know that.

All he could say to me was that we were at least four months behind in our leases, five months behind with the telephone company, three months behind in our payroll taxes, add a couple of hundred thousand dollars or so in payables—almost all of which were seriously overdue—and you could get some sense of the size of the problem.

But that wasn't all.

Creditors were complaining, he said, some were threatening to cut us off, others to sue us, we didn't have any cash, and we couldn't get a line of credit. In short, other than our continuing client receivables, we had no other source of revenue to which we could turn.

But that still wasn't all.

Our new franchisees, inexperienced and uncertain in the use of our systems, were beginning to lose clients faster than we could replace them.

Frustrated with their inability to retain clients, they were beginning to complain that our franchise didn't work.

There were rumblings out there that trouble was brewing.

Several were suggesting that there might be a legal problem in all this.

And they didn't even know the worst of it yet. None of them knew that we had run out of money.

※　※　※　※

What do you say to the woman you love when you have blown it?

When all of your ideas, your passion—your bluster, for God's sake—has exploded before you, and you are left with the mess to clean up, and you turn to look at her, and she looks back, both of you painfully silent?

What do you say then, when everything you believe to be true turns out out to be false, and she has to help you pick up the pieces?

What do you say to the woman you love when you've blown it?

What's worse, what do you say to yourself?

※　※　※　※

Ilene and I were dumbfounded.

Nothing we had ever done had prepared us for this.

We had planned everything so carefully—or so we thought.

Certainly, the company had been on an aggressive path, but that wasn't the problem. We had hit every benchmark we intended to hit, and more.

The shock wouldn't leave us. It consumed us in everything we did and trailed us everywhere we went for weeks. (Indeed, as we were to discover, the shock would trail after us for years. We still feel it today, like a thick, heavy, cloud weighing down on our shoulders, on our heads, on our relationship.) It bewildered us; it terrified us; it suffocated us; it seized our very breath. We had no idea what to do, since the problem at that point was too big to define—too complicated to understand, too sudden and overwhelming to fully comprehend.

I remember that time as a continuous stream of lunatic meetings, with our accountant, with my partner, with our accounting staff, and then back to our accountant and my partner again, and yet again, trying to make some sense out of the appalling ignorance and confusion Ilene and I encountered everywhere we went to talk about money.

They would look at each other. They would look at the floor. They would look at the ceiling, and then back at each other, and then down at their shoes. I wanted to hit them over the head, to take them by the collar, to scream at them, "What's going on with you? Don't you understand what you've done? Explain it to me! Make some sense out of this thing! Talk to me! Wake up!" But, it didn't make any difference. In the end all they did was to get angry at me!

I couldn't believe what was going on.

How could so many people who were so well-paid do so badly and be so ill-informed?

At times, when I was alone, I would explode to no one in particular in an uncontrollable fit of rage at the absolute insanity of it all! I felt so absolutely helpless!

When I would talk to our accountant, he would explain things in a calm and reasonable voice, and yet, when I looked deeper into what he said it was all so meaningless. He simply agreed with me that, yes, he and my partner and our accounting staff had screwed up, but nothing more. It was nobody's fault. We were growing so fast; we were all doing the best that anyone could given the circumstances. I can see his face even now, that dumb, bland, institutional look.

It was nobody's fault!

I could have killed him, and my partner, and our accounting manager, and all of the people who worked for them. And yet, they simply didn't seem to care!

I think that drove me crazier than anything else.

I felt like the only sane patient in an insane asylum.

Nobody's fault?

Everyone was looking at me as if *I* was the crazy one: they *indulged* me; they *understood* me; they *cared* for me; they condescended to explain things to me; but no one would admit that it was them, that it wasn't me, that there was only one explanation for our sudden condition—they were all nuts! They were literally crazy. They were certifiably insane. There was no explanation that could justify our condition, there was no rationalizing it; there was no excuse for it. It wasn't that we were growing too fast; it wasn't that our systems were "outgrown"; it wasn't that we were reaching too far. It was simply one thing and only one thing, everybody went to sleep, and they only woke up when we ran out of money!

My wife looked at me and said, "I think *we're* the crazy ones here. Let's stop for a minute and think."

※　※　※　※

January 1986 saw the beginning of what I think now of as my Education in Experts Phase.

Actually, my Education in Experts Phase is still going on today, but I'll get to that later.

In January 1986, thoroughly disgusted with my inability to achieve any clarity from the people in my company who were supposed to possess it, I brought in my first "expert" to help.

I've got to hand it to him.

It didn't take long for him to come up with a solution.

He looked at me with the most pained expression, as if to say, *how could you have done this?* (In fact, he did say that. It wasn't my imagination. His grim, grey face spoke of huge indiscretion, of massive irresponsibility, of terrible dereliction, too terrible even for him to bear!) He then told me in no uncertain terms that we had to bite the bullet, shut down the company immediately, give the business to the franchisees, and walk away, hoping that nobody found us out, hoping that I could still find a job after all I'd done—perhaps I could perform seminars on behalf of the franchisees, or maybe I could manage a sales department somewhere in the world where they hadn't heard of me yet!

He was quite emphatic about that—there was no doubt in his mind that there was absolutely no hope. I can hear his voice to this day, *no hope, no hope, no hope, no hope, no hope.*

He was the first of my no hope experts.

The others would say, "There is hope, but there's no hope unless you can afford to pay for the only hope you have. And the only hope you have is, guess what? Me!"

Meanwhile things were warming up on the franchise front.

One of our more successful franchisees—within ten months of the day he opened his doors his franchise was servicing a client base of close to 80 clients producing annualized revenue to him just under $500,000—was pressing hard for more results.

And he wanted them fast.

Why should he have to wait?

He expected to be on a million dollar course by this time!

He was working according to his own inner clock.

The business was beginning to get on his nerves.

But he did love to talk on the phone.

It seems there was nothing he loved more.

He talked to my finance department, at least once a day.

He also loved to talk to the other franchisees.

He soon became part of a chorus.

A chorus of More! More! More!

Everywhere I turned somebody was asking for more.

I couldn't blame them, actually.

If I could have waved a magic wand, I would have asked for the very same thing.

Who didn't want more?

My creditors did.

※   ※   ※   ※

Money, money, money.

Ilene and I rented an apartment in southern California to be closer to our recently opened operation there, while my partner was to focus his attention on northern California.

I flew back and forth between the two to keep score, to do seminars, to move business forward.

Under Ilene's direction, sales were growing in southern California.

In March, my partner resigned. He couldn't afford to stay on any longer.

He wrote me a long letter after he left telling me how stupid I was. I agreed with him. But for different reasons.

To bring the cost of doing business down to a tolerable level, we closed our corporate offices, cut over 30 people from our corporate payroll, and moved our remaining corporate staff into our northern California regional office across town.

Shortly after my partner resigned, I fired our accountant and our first expert (it may be my imagination, but I believe they walked out the door together—they somehow merge in my mind into one very misty grey presence—and from the back they looked like twin brothers, joined at the hip), and hired a new accounting firm to replace them, a small regional upbeat firm which had the confidence I sorely needed at the time, that if the job could get done, well, by damn, they could and would, do it!

I still can see the senior partner's face as it looked to me then. Actually, it's not that my memory is that good, but that I recently spent two weeks in court with the very same senior partner where he was suing me for what he said I owed him, and I was suing him for malpractice. I should have paid him the $30,000 he said I owed him when he first asked for it in 1986 after his firm worked our account for four months and left us in worse shape than they found us. But that was our very contention in the law suit. They didn't agree then and they don't agree now (who knows what they really think?). In fact, they won, and with attorney's fees included, the final bill came to more than $195,000! What I saw in that senior partner's eyes in March 1986 was a resolute scrapper of a man—a real killer of a guy, somebody who would really go for the throat when he felt it was called for. That's why I hired him. I thought he would go for the throat of my problem as he said he would. As it turned out, that wasn't his primary skill at all. But he sure did go for *my* throat when, after paying the first $4,000 bill, I refused to pay the balance! He didn't actually get around to suing us until 1988, after he had sold his firm to one of the Big Six accounting firms. When the final demand for payment came in early 1988, Ilene wrote him a letter explaining that, given our devastated financial condition, the only beneficiaries of litigation would be our attorneys. He responded that he would be willing to accept anything as payment, ". . . jewelry, furniture, rugs . . ." (a charming guy, a true, endearing expert, one of my favorites of all time!)

❊ ❊ ❊ ❊

Money, money, money—the conflagration grew in intensity.

Ilene and I spent more time apart than together, she in southern California, I up north. We'd talk late at night on the telephone, telling each other what was going on, what wasn't. We felt sorry for ourselves; we were angry; we were afraid; we fought. We fought with each other about fights we had with other people. We loved each other on the telephone, and then we hung up in a fit of pique. She'd call me back, and then I'd call her back, and we'd apologize to each other, only to get angry again when something, anything, triggered our sense of helplessness and rage. We went on like that, day after day, week after week, month after month. It was tearing us apart.

Every day brought a new threat, a new crisis, a new problem.

The franchisees weren't rumbling now; they were absolutely screaming threats.

Our people, too, had a problem.

What had once been such a great business it couldn't be true, was now such a bad business it couldn't be true.

To say I was losing credibility is the understatement of the decade. As each catastrophic day went by, I was quickly becoming the business pariah of the year to someone new.

"How could everything go so wrong so fast?" they would ask me. "What really happened here?"

My answers satisfied some, but failed to satisfy others.

Unfortunately, the ones who weren't satisfied weren't always the ones who left.

Sometimes, as I discovered, the ones who thought the worst of me stayed on to watch what I'd do.

I could see them out of the corner of my eye, watching me, writing things down. Was I imagining this? I don't think so, but it could be. At the time, nothing would have surprised me.

My new controller, a thin, young woman CPA my ex-accountant had recommended for the job, often came to me with complaints about our new accountants, about the people who worked for her, about the stress of working there, about life in general under the new conditions. Her face would get all pouty and drawn, her eyes moist; her lips would tremble. All I could say to her is that I was sorry; I understood what a problem everything was right now; these were trying times, but that she would have to take charge. I'm sure I didn't tell her keep a stiff upper lip, but it must have sounded like that. I wasn't making good sense to just about anyone, least of all to myself. She would nod resolutely and shuffle back to her desk, as though in her slippers! That's the only picture I have of her to this day: her face pinched, her shoulders bowed, her eyes moist and anxious about when and where all this would end. I'm certain she thought that if she continued much longer in this degraded and deteriorating financial environment her CPA badge (or whatever they call it) would be stripped from her breast forever at a meeting of her peers, that she would have to go back to the ignominy of being a lonely grunt bookkeeper in an auto parts store until she worked off the shame.

And still, no matter what we did to defend ourselves, to put things right, they kept getting worse.

If the franchisees had been angry before, they were now a mad raging horde.

My inability to respond incensed them even more.

Reasoning with them did no good. All they wanted was money.

In a moment of weakness, I felt so bad that I wrote one of them a personal check. He took it in a second, and then demanded more.

I felt as if I was locked in a room with a bunch of gangsters.

I don't know how I did it, I just kept working, trying to get things right again, trying to move out of the swamp we were in.

But the swamp was deeper than I was tall. I felt myself being sucked down, with nothing to hold onto. I was going to drown.

❊ ❊ ❊ ❊

Money, money, money.

I fired my second accountants and our controller and hired a third expert with experience up and down his arm to replace them.

Dan was a godsend.

He took charge of our problem in a minute.

Everything settled down.

First there was confusion, and then there wasn't.

I couldn't believe it!

He was either one hell of a professional financial manager as his credentials and his references professed him to be, or a hypnotist! I couldn't be sure, but to be honest, I didn't really care.

At least there was a clear division between the front lines and where we worked. The shells stopped going off in the middle of the office. The front lines were on the other side of the telephone, on the other side of the door, out there somewhere, somewhere where we weren't, and Dan and our people were in here, settling down, getting our house in order, making things nice.

He had such a calm and settled air about him!

"What about . . .?" I would ask him.

"It's handled," he'd say.

Could this be true?

He would prove it.

Could things be finally shifting? I would wonder to myself aloud.

He would reassure me.

I became a true believer. I took my newfound treasure, my financial maven, the proof of my sanity, my new guy called Dan, to southern California with me to show him off to the franchisees.

Dan and I prepared ourselves.

We had a strategy.

He was going to show them how much we were prepared to do.

We had reports drawn up to show them the truth.

We were going to dispel the rumors once and for all. We were going to show them, finally, how everything was moving in the right direction, how Ilene's extraordinary efforts were really paying off, that sales were increasing to the point where all of us soon would be in tip top shape. Everything was going to be alright—you'll see. Show them Dan.

Dan showed them, but they didn't like him either.

They got angrier and angrier.

They followed us down the hall as we left the meeting.

If they had had feathers and tar they would have used them.

Nothing would satisfy them.

The worm had turned.

Only blood would do.

* * * *

But, even then, Dan was unfrazzled.

Not me—I was a wreck.

Every place I went I felt like a criminal.

And, for the life of me, I had done nothing wrong!

I couldn't go to bed without hearing taunts.

My imagination was working overtime.

The embarrassment was unbearable.

I gave seminars almost every day, trainings with my people, spoke to Ilene every night. On the outside I spoke about mastering business; on the inside I quaked in my boots.

To make matters even worse, my first book, *The E-Myth,* was beginning to take off. People were calling. They admired my work. They professed undying gratitude, adoration. They had never thought about their business that way; my point of view about business was directly to the point; it touched them where they lived; I knew of what I spoke. They didn't know the half of it. I was dying a thousand deaths every day. My book stuck in my craw. I wished I could undo it, make it go away until I was ready, until I got everything back under control as we had had it before the book came out.

Did I see the hint of a smile on Dan's face then?

Was my zen master of a financial maven ruminating about the strange twists of my fate?

Did he see some kharmic rectitude in what was going down?

Did he want to help it along somehow, just to ease my pain?

❋　❋　❋　❋

Money, money, money.

My first expert sued me for $5,000. When the complaint was served, the person on our finance staff who received it gave it to Dan. He ignored it. Undisputed, my first expert got a default judgment, and as swift as a mouse, swooped the five grand from our bank account.

His twin brother, my first accountant, got wind of how easy it was. He sued me for more than $20,000. The same employee gave the new complaint to Dan, which he ignored as well. Ditto, my first accountant followed his twin brother's suit, and grabbed twenty-two big ones from our now trembling account. Dan didn't flinch. At least not so I could notice. After all, *he* didn't create the problem, *I* did, the author, who was going to be famous, who was going to teach people how to avoid such problems. It was *my* expert, it was *my* accountant, and there was a lesson in all this. "Pay your bills!" he almost said.

❋　❋　❋　❋

How can a business work and not work at the same time?

I can prove to you it's easy.

I can prove to you that in a moment of sleep, or inattention, or distraction it can all come down around your ears.

Have I been too hard on myself? Not hard enough.

Or, perhaps, you think I have let myself off the hook, that I am focusing too much blame on my first accountant, on my partner, on my first expert, on my controller, on my second accountants, on my franchisees, on Dan?

Perhaps you've already lost so much faith in my credibility that you're wondering, what could I possibly say now that could make a difference? What in the world could I possibly teach you now about business? How could anyone make such a royal mess of things?

What is heroic in all this? What is worth learning in all this? Could you show this to your son and daughter studying for their M.B.A.?

I can see my saxophone teacher, Merle, smiling in his grave. I can see my uncle Al, chuckling mirthlessly to himself, I told you so, as he monitored my progress in business with a baleful, experienced, jaundiced, and hopelessly cynical eye! You dummy! You ignoramous! You let yourself get caught!

I can see my editor, my publisher, reading this manuscript for the very first time, asking themselves, how is he going to get out of this one? Have we tied ourselves to a nut? Is this going to work out? Is there some surprise he's waiting to spring—aha!—a turnaround, a sleight of hand, an entrepreneurial tour de force, a denouement, a subtle gesture, a wonderful *voila!* and that's that?

How does he get out of this one, folks?

What is the Financial Ideal?

How can a business work and not work at the same time?

※　※　※　※

Ilene grew our business in southern California from a dead start to an annualized rate of $2,000,000 in gross revenues in one year.

The system I created worked.

She worked the system, and the system worked.

She then came back to northern California, fired Dan, and took over the finance department.

I never saw Dan again.

※　※　※　※

I forgot to tell you, before Ilene came home, a few other things happened. Not necessarily in the following order.

We received our first franchise rescission.

What that means is that a franchisee took *our* name off of his door, put *his* name on it, took *our* copyright off of *our* materials, put *his* copyright on them, notified the clients we gave to him to begin paying *him* directly rather than *us,* and in one fell swoop immediately siphoned close to $60,000 a month out of our pocket!

That's right, you heard me, the guy who liked to make phone calls, who loved to talk to franchisees every day—the guy who got my personal check, the guy who stood over me one day and told me something bad was about to happen, leaned down over my desk, hovered there over my shining, palpitating head, swore very quietly in a voice so stern, so solemn, so sinister, that something unimaginably bad was going to happen, *the guy whose business was growing through the damn roof,* the guy you would think would be the last to be concerned about anything, the guy who swore up and down that he only meant the very best—that very same guy rescinded his franchise agreement!

And the most extraordinary thing about it is he's still doing business to this very day!

But, that's not all.

Five more franchisees followed suit.

Hundreds of thousands of dollars stopped flowing into our company—just went away with a snap of the fingers.

Devastation upon devastation.

Was God trying to tell me something?

Was Dan right?

Was there a message in all this?

What did Ilene and Michael do for goodness sake?

What would *you* have done?

※ ※ ※ ※

Money, money, money.

I was told a story recently of a franchisor who was threatened with a revolt by his franchisees, went to the leader of the revolt, asked to see him in private, took him by the tie, pulled him to his face, and told him that if he persisted in creating chaos he was going to have him *killed!*

I don't necessarily believe this story, but I can understand it!

When you are under attack, strange things happen inside.

When you are under attack, you either get your balance or you don't.

If you don't, you keep falling backwards until you're on your back.

For almost a year and a half I teetered on the edge of falling.

I was dealing with so many dissonant forces, so many malevolent surprises, so many negative people, that I couldn't catch my breath.

I had never known, had never even imagined, the overwhelming force that money could create.

If I had fallen, I know that I never would have gotten up again.

If I had let go for just one minute, I would have found it impossible to regain my balance.

If I had allowed myself to believe what I was being told—what people were saying about me—I never would have been able to stand up again in front of a small business owner and speak my piece with any conviction.

If I had not caught myself in time, I would have never learned the lesson I am about to share with you.

But, before I share *it* with you, there's more to tell.

❋ ❋ ❋ ❋

One Friday night, when I was fourteen, I was walking home from a football game with a close friend. Three men were walking behind us, but we didn't think anything of it; they were probably also walking home from the game. My friend and I were talking about nothing in particular, when suddenly the three men were on us. One of them held a knife to my throat and told me not to say a word. The second man held a knife to my friend's stomach and told him not to move. The third man then proceeded to beat the living hell out of my friend with his fists. It was over as fast as it began. The three men ran away, and my friend and I went home.

For whatever reason, my friend and I didn't see each other much after that night. After a short time, we stopped seeing each other altogether.

I didn't know why then, but I think I know why now.

We were both so ashamed.

※   ※   ※   ※

1987 saw the beginning of a new wave of threats.

We now had a new accountant; Ilene was in charge of finance; we were truly getting our financial house in order; and then the lawsuits began in earnest.

We were sued for fraud. We were sued for misrepresentation. We were sued for violations of the franchise laws. We were sued for everything they could think of. We were sued for enormous amounts of money.

We found ourselves a legal firm that came highly recommended.

Our first meeting included three attorneys, my wife Ilene, and I.

We familiarized them with our problem.

It took us about three hours to discuss the ramifications.

That first meeting cost us about $1,600 dollars, one hundred and seventy five dollars an hour per attorney times three hours.

They told us we had a problem, but we were in the right.

I told them that I knew both of those things to be true, but still we had a problem, and it didn't seem to make much difference that we were in the right.

They nodded, knowing how we must feel, but that was the way the world worked, the way the cookie crumbled, the way the dice fell, the way our fortune looked. Besides which, they said, we didn't have much of a choice, our franchisees were suing us, we hadn't initiated the suits.

In retrospect, I know we should have stopped everything right then, but naturally we couldn't. We were in it up to our ears. We simply didn't believe it could get any worse.

But, naturally, it did—much worse.

If our business had been a war zone before, we were now under atomic attack. All of the light weapons had been used up, major explosions were the normal course of every day. We'd arrive at the office—major explosion. We'd stop to eat lunch—major explosion. Ilene, our people, and I were suffering from shell shock, but somehow we went on.

The legal bills mounted. Yet the war persisted, it didn't care about cost. Cost was irrelevant here; cost was always the last thing to be considered; cost was always something that occurred *after* a shot was fired, *after* a bomb was dropped; cost was what the law exacted from us for not having gone to law school ourselves, for not being accountants ourselves, for not knowing enough to answer the questions at the risk of more cost. Cost was never planned during those grim days; it was always the price of a shock.

Over the next four years of unlikely, unimaginable, indecent events, our legal fees alone came to over $500,000! They simply added up: an hour here, a telephone call there, a marathon meeting here, a court appearance there. All we could do was defend ourselves. Not once did we go on the offensive; not once did we develop enough traction on the legal front to turn the tide our way. And we had the very best legal help money could buy. Our guys were known in the legal community as good. They said they knew what had to be done, but our financial condition wouldn't allow them, or us, to do it. (It continued to come as a surprise to me that while our financial condition continually prevented us from going on the offensive, it didn't prevent the bills from adding up!)

A prevailing sense of injustice dogged our every step.

What was illegal for the opposition to do they did with impunity.

What was legal for us to do, became, for the most arcane reasons under the sun, impossible to do.

There were reasons, of course.

The reasons sounded quite judicious, but only for a second.

                    ⁕   ⁕   ⁕   ⁕

It didn't happen with a loud click or strike us with a sudden trumpet blare, but somewhere along the way something shifted, something gave, and Ilene and I buckled down for the long haul.

We suddenly came to the realization that this simply wasn't going to go away; that it was going to take a long, long while, and a lot of money, to turn around.

We sold our home and put the money into the business.

We stopped paying ourselves and lived on my speaking engagements and royalties.

We created payment schedules for the more than 100 creditors who were waiting in line, grousing at the door, calling us every day for money we didn't have.

The schedules extended for years in some cases.

And yet, our creditors accepted our terms.

When Dan was there, he had hung up on them.

When our second accountants were there, they had made promises they didn't keep if they talked to them at all, which in most cases they didn't.

Ilene, God bless her, made promises, and then began to keep them, week after week, month after month, year after year.

She was committed to keeping her word, and did most of the time.

But still, there was the need to produce the money to keep our promises, and the company's revenue was shrinking around our ears.

Our remaining franchisees were losing clients so fast that it was beginning to have a profoundly negative impact on our marketing people.

Who wants to sell something they don't trust?

Sales began to slide precipitously.

We rallied our people together; cut back on anything we could, again and again, and then cut back even more, to bring the company down to a financially manageable size; gained commitments from our people to help us to pull the company out of its tailspin; called in what chips we had; and found out that there were many chips we didn't even know about.

What we found out is that most of our people cared. They wanted to be included. They wanted to join the fight. They knew we somehow had blundered into a tornado but they also trusted that we could find a way out.

They thought our business was more than worthwhile.

That it was worth whatever effort it took.

Those who couldn't handle the chaos, the disruption, the negative forces, left to do something else. There were some teary goodbyes.

Those leaving and those left behind felt an incomparable sense of loss.

Ilene and I developed a financial strategy to buy back as many of the remaining franchises as we could in order to save the remaining clients and work with them ourselves as we had before we began to franchise.

We knew we could keep the clients, and we knew that that would have a marked impact on our marketing, client services, and finance people. Clients produce cash flow, and cash flow was critical. But becoming a trusted business and producing results our people could be proud of was even more critical.

Our negotiations with the franchisees were anything but easy. We didn't have any cash, so the only way we could buy their businesses was with a note and payments extending far into the future.

One by one most finally accepted our offers. We bought their businesses, and even negotiated settlements with the landlords of the franchisees who had continuing lease obligations, so they could be free to walk away.

The other part of our strategy was to restrict our interactions with our clients to telephone, fax, and mail.

Everyone said that the strategy would fail.

In such a "high-touch" business as ours, people would say, the client must see the consultant if the relationship is to work.

I didn't think so.

My experience had shown me that the telephone could be an incredibly intimate instrument. One can communicate and interact powerfully on the telephone; it is an incredibly effective teaching tool if used well.

Without the distraction of the visual, the voice takes a central place, becomes a stronger medium, and as the voice becomes central to communication, the ability to listen becomes significantly more important as well.

It was my contention that by restricting our interaction with our clients to the telephone the experience wouldn't suffer, but, to the contrary, would flourish.

In any case it was a moot point.

If we were to stay alive we had to rescue our clients from our franchisees, and to rescue the clients we had to work with them long distance. We had no other choice.

And it worked!

Our client retention soared. Our productivity per client increased dramatically. Our profitability per client was substantially improved. And, best of all, our control over the entire client relationship increased exponentially.

Finally, we were turning things around.

We were pulling things out of the fire.

Our first real strategy since the tornado struck was beginning to pay off.

The only problem was that between the 100 creditors and the franchises we had agreed to buy back, Ilene and I had now incurred over $2 million we had to pay off!

※　※　※　※

Money, money, money.

The anger over money-gone-wrong knows no bounds.

If there is an ugly side to anyone—and there is, believe me, I've seen it at its virulent worst—there is nothing like money-gone-wrong to bring it out.

If you've never seen that part of a person, you should count your blessings.

It is a demon from hell!

His little eyes flash red and yellow with fire; his little teeth grind unmercifully, gnashing, gnashing, in the hope of red meat; his little fingers scratch and tear at anything within reach—for clumps of hair or for the crotch of your pants, they pull viciously at doors, at drawers, looking for the money, knowing it's hiding, knowing you're hiding it, knowing they're being deprived of their FOOD! Those little dark demons are built out of wire, steel, bone, muscle, gristle and stone. Their flesh only appears to be flesh, it is in fact only wax with hair; their expressions and features constantly change in the heat of the moment from grimaces to grins to sneers to rage to lust. They are not real, but evil spirits brought up from the deep, from the bowels of the earth, brought forth to maim, to fester, to annihilate, to scream bloody murder, bloody loss, to foul the air with their blasphemous bleatings and complaints, to tear and rend things apart until they can't be put back together again, to destroy until nothing is left, until nothing is recognizable by either family or friend.

At least that's what it seemed they were trying to do to us.

They were trying to eviscerate us.

Every time I saw one of the six franchisees who were on the offensive (I thought of them as the offensive six), their faces grew darker, black, red, and purple; their eyes took on a yellow unhealthy cast; their mouths a perpetual snarl, filled with venom. They wanted everyone to know what an evil soul I was, that had they not met me their lives would be complete; prior to becoming franchisees every-thing was set for them, their paths were clear—they knew the cherry blossoms every spring, the rich red and yellow leaves of a Connecticut fall—their lives had been exemplary examples of fiscal, spiritual, and familial responsibility. Now, due to me—they had nothing to do with it: they were innocent victims of a diabolical scheme—their lives were destroyed. They were going to get even—oh you better believe it, brother—they were going to get even. They were going to have my soul for lunch!

Had they been as resourceful and as dedicated to the operation of their franchises, we would never have had a problem. But, that was too much to ask.

It wasn't too long before the District Attorney called. *"Who?"* I asked my assistant.

"You heard me, the District Attorney!" she squealed, *"The goddamned D.A.!"* she screamed in a harsh whisper.

Her eyes looked like they were about to close permanently.

The D.A.?, I thought to myself. The District Attorney! I couldn't believe my ears! Was this going to become a television series? Was Judge Wapner going to call, too?

I couldn't bear the thought of what would happen next.

I had my attorney talk to him. I couldn't even imagine what I could possibly say.

Would he lean me up against my car? Would he tie chains to my arms and legs and walk me into court in front of all my clients, my children, my employees, the Chamber of Commerce, the Trucking Association?

Would I be forced to make a public apology to everyone I had ever delivered a seminar to?

Would I be forced to take back everything I had ever said?

Would the headlines in *The San Francisco Chronicle* scream out FRAUD! FRAUD! FRAUD! with my picture on the front page, my blue suit jacket pulled over my head, my arms shackled behind my back?

My attorney told me that the D.A. had received a complaint from one of our franchisees and had been investigating the complaint for several months. He had talked to quite a few people who had a lot to say about us, about me, and about our little problem. He had to decide whether or not to indict us for criminal fraud. According to our franchisee there was absolutely no question about it, indict us he should; we were as guilty as sin. We had stolen huge amounts of money—the franchisee told him—this was a major crime: millions had been stashed away in a Swiss bank; we were living a royal life style—large cars, jet setting, taking from the little people what was rightfully theirs, and using it for our own insatiably greedy and multifarious ends.

As my attorney recounted his conversation with the D.A., I could see that the ugly little demons were having a field day. I could hear their teeth gnashing on the other end of the phone. I could see them standing on the D.A.'s shoulders, whispering in his ears, swinging from his tie, playing lacrosse in his hair. I could smell their fetid breath through the telephone, burning my eyes, tearing at my lungs, forcing me to hold my breath.

The D.A. didn't sound as if he had to be pushed much further, my attorney said.

It sounded as if the cell doors were already being oiled to close.

It sounded as if he was beginning to enjoy the little fellows who were whispering in his ear by now.

The D.A. said he was really getting into white collar crime.

It was about time guys like me got what we deserved.

He sounded as if he was really interested in what this might turn out to be. It was either his lips I heard smacking on the other end of the line or the little devils lapping at the receiver.

As for me, I was about to pass out.

❋   ❋   ❋   ❋

We reached an agreement with the D.A.

We told him that he could send his auditors into our company to look for any evidence of misdeed, of fraud, of misrepresentation, of evil.

We told him we had done nothing wrong; that our business did work; that the franchisees were simply being impatient; that no one had bilked them out of their hard-earned savings; that no one had bilked them out of anything; that they were simply being assholes! We could prove it all if we could simply get our day in court.

Come on in, we said, take a close look. Look as long as you like; we've got nothing to hide.

So they did.

The D.A.'s auditors had themselves a field day.

What was supposed to take 45 to 60 days at most, took almost 9 months!

They dug into everything they could lay their hands on, and then they dug into it again. We gave them everything we had.

And they found nothing, because there *was* nothing.

But it didn't stop there.

Having found nothing, we felt it was only reasonable that the D.A. officially say so, and that he drop the case.

We had cooperated in every way he asked us to. We thought that it was only fair that he cooperate with us now.

But, that was unreasonable of us to expect.

In his last conversation with my attorney, the D.A. said that he had found something. It wasn't anything specific but there was enough there to build a healthy, incriminating, career-crushing case! Of course, he wasn't saying what it was he had found, but if we didn't toe the invisible line, he would file an indictment to do the talking for him! Unless of course we worked out our differences with the complainants—the franchisees. If we were to do that, he said pointedly, he probably wouldn't indict us—though, understand, there was no guarantee. But if we were to cooperate just a little bit more, he wouldn't pursue what was obviously to him *a criminal matter of the most egregious sort!*

"What did he say?" I asked my attorney.

"He said you're guilty," my attorney answered.

"But, why? What did he find? What reason did he give?" I almost screamed.

"He didn't say," my attorney responded.

"Then where are we now?" I asked.

"The same place we were before," my attorney admitted.

Not exactly true, I thought to myself. This has cost us a bundle.

* * * *

Money, money, money.

Our costs ran up; our money ran down. Every dime we made went to pay off our debt.

Ilene and I borrowed more money, from family, from personal lines of credit; all of it went into the business, to keep it running, to keep it from evaporating into thin air.

We created financial and operational controls so tight that the business couldn't squeak without us knowing it.

The business was insolvent, but it wasn't bankrupt. We were moving along.

Our new accountant, Dale Irwin, was a wonder.

Finally, a professional worthy of the name.

He worked with us, trusted us, developed our understanding, taught us, nurtured us, supported us in every way he could, and then went even further. When we couldn't pay him in full, he cut us some slack.

He was intimately familiar with everything that went on in our business, and he stood in awe of it.

There wasn't a day that went by when he didn't tell us how remarkable our business was, how extraordinary it had to be to have weathered such a continued and malevolent attack on all fronts. "Hang in there," he said, "it's going to work out." "Don't worry," he said, "the worst of it is behind you. We'll get it handled," he said, and damn if we didn't.

Day after day, an hour at a time, whittling it, molding it, coddling it, nursing it, helping it along—we faced the unfaceable and came through it so many times that we began to regain our former optimism.

Our people grew smarter, deeper, richer, and more persistent.

They learned to fight off the hounds. They learned to get what they needed. They learned that the world isn't always a safe place to be, but that you could make it safer if you had heart, discipline, a long lance, and good armor.

They learned that money was nothing to fool around with. It had a will all its own.

✳   ✳   ✳   ✳

A word about money.

I have heard so many new-age would-be business mavens repeat that saddest of noxious platitudes, "Do the right things and the money will take care of itself." Let me tell you this, the money *never* takes care of itself! *Never.*

I have learned the hard way, and continue to learn, that the money—the food of a business—must be tended to constantly.

Daily.

Not monthly; not annually; but daily.

By the hour is best.

I have learned that everyone has a different perception of money—ingests money, digests money, values money, in a totally subjective and very personal way. Employees. Customers. Suppliers. Lenders.

Don't screw around with those perceptions!

You will lose a hand!

And if you persist, you'll lose more than that.

In a Free Market System, money is the measure.

In a Free Market System, money speaks.

In a Free Market System, we have been taught only too well that what we own is who we are. And what we own is the byproduct of money.

Don't mess with that truth.

Don't even think you can mess with that truth.

The minute you mess with that truth—no matter what you believe to be true about the person whose money you're messing around with—that person will have your head.

He won't intend to, mind you.

He wouldn't believe it of himself.

But he will do it all the same!

He will eat your head for lunch!

Please don't call me cynical. I'm not.

Please don't send me letters proving me wrong, that you have an example of how wrong I can be.

Please don't bother, I'm sure there are exceptions to the rule.

There always are.

But the rule is the rule nonetheless.

Mess around with peoples' money in a Free Market System, and your goose is cooked.

Even if you didn't do it, they'll say you did.

Even if you did do it, but didn't intend to, you're name is still mud.

Even if you only thought about doing it, the wrath will descend upon you as though from the hand of God.

In a Free Market System, money is a monstrously complicated thing.

It is all some people have.

It is all some people are.

It is all some people want.

It is what lies down beside them in bed at night.

It is how they value their day.

If they think they have a right to it they will kill you for it.

If they think that it is scarce they will hoard it away.

If they think that they are in danger of losing what they have they will buy a handgun and run away to the hills to protect it.

If they believe it is sexy they will make love to it.

If they believe it is power they will make a club of it and beat you senseless until you give way.

If they believe it will keep them safe they will dress themselves in it.

In a Free Market System money is the only thing that stands between most people and the awful, bottomless, terrifying void.

❋　❋　❋　❋

Well, I'm sure you want to know what happened.

I'm sure you want to know the end of the story.

I wish I could tell you, but I can't.

Because, so far, there is no end.

So far, Ilene and I have paid off $1 million of our $2 million debt.

Our business is still producing remarkable results for our clients.

We have never missed a payroll during this entire madcap time, and we're proud of that.

We own very little, owe a great deal, and continue to struggle with the imponderable.

The D.A. hasn't called back, but I'm sure he's still there. Sometimes I can feel his breath at the back of my ears.

And, every day we win two and lose one. The continuing sense of forward movement only validates the decision we made in 1986 to make things right.

Somehow, we have not lost our drive to overcome all of this. In fact, we have found in this experience the depths of our drive, something we never would have discovered had life been kinder.

There is a positive energy that continues to fuel our day, an extraordinary vitality which grows in us almost by the hour as we witness the minor miracles that occur as a result of our persistence, our determination, our love of what we do, our appreciation of those who have supported us, our unrelenting vision.

This has been, to Ilene and me, an exceptional opportunity, a rite of passage, an odyssey of heroic proportions. I wouldn't trade it for the world.

$1 million more to go we say to each other, Ilene and I.

$1 million more to go.

Why do we do it?

What's the point of all this?

Well, let me answer that in the following way.

Ilene received this letter just the other day from a client she personally worked with, one of the thousands we've worked with over the years:

Dear Ilene:
As October draws near, I realize that my life has come in a full circle. It has been 24 months since you and I began the turnaround process of my business. I am well pleased to see that the pain and suffering in the beginning have become satisfaction and a deep sense of pride and well-being two years later.

The most recent accomplishment that sealed the circle was that, after selling our home a year and a half ago to help save our sickly business, in June we purchased a house. Not just any house, but a wonderful, large four bedroom home by the sea, which overlooks the Montara mountains and has a view of the ocean.

It is a place to raise my children and to live in happiness, and I love every part of it. Every time I drive to it, or away from it, I think to myself that I must live in the most beautiful place in the whole world.

Of course, my life still has its highs and lows and everyday problems and frustrations, but I am pleased with the progress I have made and I take things in stride.

This brings me to the point of my letter. Enclosed is a very small Thank You gift. It is especially small, when one considers the enormous amount of help you gave me two years ago. Without all your help, the lessons you taught me, and the 'life gifts' I received from you, I would never have been sitting here writing you today, and my business would have been bankrupt.

Please know that this gift comes from my heart, and it represents the first half of the circle which you helped me achieve.

I shall always admire you and think only the kindest thoughts about you.

You have much to be proud of, Ilene.

Very truly yours,

Laura C. Strom, C.F.O.
Heirloom Engravers

That's why we've done it, that's why we continue to do it.

And, after all, as our accountant Dale Irwin would say in his own, inimitable, deep-hearted way,

"You've only got $1 million more to go."

"By God, you're half way there!"

8.
THE POWER POINT PERSPECTIVE

Consciousness *and* Conscience *are similar in
their respective spheres, one being in the*
Intellectual Center, *the other in the* Emotional
Center. *Consciousness is* Knowing *all together;*
Conscience is Feeling *all together.*

—*Maurice Nicoll*
Psychological Commentaries

I'm sure that countless businesses in this country have responded enthusiastically over the past decade to the clarion call for a return to those worthwhile puritan values of *service, excellence,* and *caring.* To the creation of "mission statements," and the nurturing of their "corporate culture".

You know who you are.

Unfortunately, I'm also sure that, despite the initial fervor such clarion calls create, most of these businesses operate the same way today as they did before the flag was raised, with equally slipshod service, mediocre performance, and as greedy and self-serving a mind-set as ever.

That's because neither service, excellence, nor caring can be produced by executive fiat, or by wishing it so.

Tom Peters can rail all he wants. It won't make any difference.

The adoption of service, excellence, and caring as strategic options— as slogans—to revive a dead or dying business is not only antithetical to the true meaning of those words, but as cynical as anything our Machiavellian minds can produce: in short, it won't work.

146

Service, excellence, and caring are not something you can do anything about. They are a state of mind.

When a business is bereft of such qualities, it is because its founders, its owners, and its managers are bereft of such qualities.

They don't care to serve.

It doesn't bother them that their performance is less, by far, than excellent.

They don't care about the business because they simply don't care at all.

That's why such words fail to work for them, indeed for most companies who attempt to adopt them for their own purposes, to their own strategic ends.

Because the cynical use of true human values always produces exactly the opposite of what was intended.

True human values cannot be adopted for the expedient or the pragmatic. They are not "tools" with which to develop a "management style."

They are *values.* They are beliefs. They are how one views the world. They are either a part of us, or they're not.

They cannot be tried on like a suit, the right color, the right shape.

They are not there to be used.

They can't be.

They won't tolerate it.

There is something fundamentally obscene about even trying to.

So to create a Power Point company, you—the founders, the owners, and the managers of companies everywhere—must already possess a Power Point Perspective.

And, if you don't already have one, you're in deep, deep trouble.

❆   ❆   ❆   ❆

Those who possess a Power Point Perspective are what I would call Pragmatic Idealists.

They are never happy with anything less than perfection, but they measure perfection by its unparalleled ability to produce practical results in the world.

Pragmatic Idealists are not sentimental.

They are driven.

They are not patient.

They are often unkind.

Pragmatic Idealists do not pander to the comfort zone in people, they do not make it easy for people to get by.

My saxophone teacher was a Pragmatic Idealist.

He lived in a world of perfection.

But he practiced achieving it in this world.

He could hear the perfect tone in his head.

He could imagine the perfect scale.

I doubt that he ever was satisfied, however, with any of his students, or with himself.

Yet he loved what he did, and what they did. It was his passion and his paradox.

He would listen to Charlie Parker with awe, and yet he could hear every flaw, every inarticulate statement, every failure to touch the sublime, the perfect, the absolute.

And as much as he held Charlie Parker in awe, Merle could not forgive him for his indifference, for his lassitude, for his unwillingness to give it his all.

And that is the dark conflict—that exquisite, yet tragic, tension between the possible and the impossible—that lives within Pragmatic Idealists.

They are hopelessly stuck in a less than perfect world, in a world in which most people quit long before Pragmatic Idealists even get started. Yet, it is not other people who drive Pragmatic Idealists to desperation, who are continued disappointments, it is they who disappoint themselves most of all. They are forever lost in their own failings. As good as they are, they are never good enough—never smart enough, never disciplined enough, never sensitive enough. Yet, in their minds, they are always on the edge of something—a breakthrough, a discovery, a find of existential importance.

Pragmatic Idealists in business know what the drive for excellence is all about. They invented it. They are its slaves. They cannot imagine any other way to live. Excellence is not a word to them. It is not a strategy, but a feeling, a passion—a profound idea. It courses through their veins.

I'm talking about tough stuff.

I'm suggesting that great companies become great companies because they are headed by great people who don't feel their greatness, *and never will!*

Great companies, Power Point companies, are headed by great people who are possessed by a burning hunger to create something perfect in the world that they can't find in themselves.

And they can't help themselves!

It's not something they do out of choice.

They are completely possessed.

They are caught up by an idea which continually eludes them, which hovers tantalizingly just out of reach, which can't be perfectly seen or apprehended, but which promises to reveal itself at any moment if the seeker will just extend him or herself one step more.

In other words, the Power Point Perspective, the desire to create a great company, or a great saxophonist, or a great automobile, or a great garden, is not for the fainthearted, the weak, or the sentimental.

It takes everything one has, and more.

It is both a blessing and a curse.

❄ ❄ ❄ ❄

Understand, I'm not talking about heroes here.

Most often, these people are unbearable to be around.

If they are impeccable in one thing, they are often disasters in another.

They are walking contradictions.

Rink Babka, for over two decades one of the top ten discus throwers in the world, told me that his coach, Dink Templeton, one of the most brilliant coaches the world has ever known, "smoked like a chimney, drank like a fish, and swore like a trooper." Yet, when it came to the sport, there was no one more dedicated, more possessed, more committed to perfection for his boys.

It is no secret that Walt Disney was a dope when it came to business finance; if it had been left up to him his business would have failed a dozen times.

It is no secret that Ross Perot is a megalomaniac, ego-ridden and paternalistic, not really one of the boys.

It is no secret that Ray Kroc held permanent grudges, insulted his people, and was known to throw fits of temper like the worst adolescent.

And yet, while all these things are true, there is a brilliance about such people—a vital edge which distinguishes them from everyone else. You can see it in their eyes.

That vital edge comes from the fact that they are driven by ideas.

Ideas reside at the heart of the Power Point Perspective.

Those who are possessed by the Power Point Perspective are driven by ideas.

Ideas are the food by which such people are nourished, revitalized, and given the life they crave—ideas of such awesome size, temper, and quality, that they are compelled to recreate them, to give them physical form, to give them presence, to give them substance, to give them reality in this world.

❉   ❉   ❉   ❉

Discussing his novel, *A Good Day to Die,* author Jim Harrison explains that the title was borrowed from Indian lore.

That comes from the Nez Perce saying, the whole idea you have to be morally and spiritually, as a warrior—whether you're a writer or businessman—you have to live so correctly that you can wake up in the morning and look out and say, "Today is a good day to die." One very rarely is in that kind of shape, but it's a tremendous thing to be able to say.[1]

How many of us could wake up and say, "Today is a good day to die"?

How many of us have lived "morally and spiritually as a warrior"?

How many of us have lived so correctly, that we could, if faced with death, let go of our lives without regret, completely empty, devoid of shame, regret, longing?

What does it mean to live correctly?

What would a warrior businessman, a warrior merchant, be?

※　※　※　※

It's not the business at all.

The whole idea falls apart if it's tied down by a business.

The whole idea becomes unthinkable if it's tied down by the idea of Cheez Balls, or Ritz Crackers, or Jello.

The whole idea of the Power Point Perspective isn't tied down to the commercial reality of what our business is doing, it exceeds it.

It raises it up.

A Power Point company doesn't make Cheez Balls.

1. *Vis-à-Vis* (United Airlines inflight magazine), October 1990.

Because Cheez Balls are not something a person can feel good about.

No matter how hard he or she tries.

And, if he or she could feel good about Cheez Balls, it's already too late!

No, if there could be such a person as a warrior merchant (and we're just pursuing possibilities here), I would imagine that he or she would be able to discriminate between Cheez Balls and other more worthwhile things.

An essential component of the Power Point Perspective is that what a business creates—the commodities or products it sells or chooses to develop for sale—is critical to the values inherent in the business itself.

Because making Cheez Balls has no inherent value, and is of value only because of the money it creates, and because creating money by making Cheez Balls must ultimately degrade one's dignity—one's sense of personal human value—the warrior merchant we are speaking about (if there could be such a person) could not live in such a state. He or she would not wish to be found by death in such a state. It most certainly would not be "a good day to die" if that were the case.

How could anybody choose Cheez Balls as their intentional fate?

❊   ❊   ❊   ❊

I've watched an iron man win the Iron Man contest.

I've watched a slight, wiry woman climb straight up a mountain.

I've watched a monster of a man win the Heavyweight title by soundly whipping a mansized monster.

I've watched a whip-fast master defeat another whip-fast master with one stroke in Karate.

I've watched a master violinist hold an audience in thrall.

On the other hand, I've watched Marino Santos use more of himself, while touching more people more permanently than any one of these five ever did or ever would.

And yet, to the world any one of the five might be considered more noble than Marino Santos, because their efforts would be considered to be more worthwhile.

I disagree.

I believe that Marino Santos invented a new paradigm of service for the world.

I believe he heroically exceeded the limits imposed by the existing paradigm, and, in the process, by being diligent, conscientious, interested, deliberate, and intelligent, holds the potential to positively affect—if all else goes right—the emotions, standards, behavior, and the quality of life, of millions of people by his example of doing ordinary work in such an extraordinary way.

I believe he took more of himself to task than most people ever will. He extended what he found to the outside world, creating a new model of behavior, a new rigor of attention, a new level of consciousness, both intense and relaxed all at the same time.

I know in my heart that Marino Santos would never make Cheez Balls.

You know it too.

❊   ❊   ❊   ❊

There must have been a moment in time at the beginning of the Free Market System, when the human mind and the human heart were asked, "Cheez Balls or not, what do you think?"

And the human being responded, "Screw it, Cheez Balls it is."

A moment when something unoffensively trivial inserted itself into the human equation as significantly more important than it was. When something much less trivial—something so big in us we couldn't get our arms around it—found no justification for hanging around, so we sat down on the sidelines stuffing Cheez Balls into our faces instead. They were so easy, so available, so tasty—so dead.

What is it about us that makes it so easy to be so self-indulgent?

What is it about a Free Market System that seems to breed Cheez Balls like flies?

What is it about us in a Free Market System that never grows tired of yet another variation on the Cheez Balls theme, whether we're poets, philosophers, mathematical giants, computer programmers, dentists, doctors, college professors, truck drivers, or poodle clippers?

In a Free Market System somehow "Pass the Cheez Balls, please!" always wins the day.

❅   ❅   ❅   ❅

But, wait a second, Cheez Balls aren't the problem!

It's this thing about dying.

It's this thing about always being prepared to die today.

It's about having lived so impeccably, having lived so correctly, having carried oneself with such presence, such dignity, having lived with such awareness, such inner vitality, such grace, such intensity as if "a fire were raging in your hair."

It's our choice of being that's the problem.

It's that which separates the Power Point business from all the others.

It's the warrior merchant's penchant for living in a state of grace.

※   ※   ※   ※

I know a man who can sell anything, and has.

I'll call him Murray, but that's not his name, he knows who he is if he is reading this.

There is something about Murray which disturbs me.

He has the eye of a pirate. You know what I mean: it has a certain slant to it. It shines like a hard black stone caught just right in the sun—as if you could walk the plank for all he cares; it has nothing to do with him.

Yet, Murray believes he is exactly the opposite of that.

Murray believes in himself and what he does.

Murray is all business, and business is all Murray.

As I said, he can sell anything, and has.

To Murray there is no difference between things.

He is totally devoid of values.

But he doesn't believe that about himself.

He believes he has values; he talks about them all the time.

He believes that he is a scientist, that he truly understands what people want.

That he is a scientist of the passions.

He has made a study of them. He has discovered the words to use to provide people with what he believes they want. He has discovered the way to provide people with the illusion that they're getting what they want. He has found a way to believe that what he does is important. Murray is a magician.

He sells this service to people. He calls it Marketing.

Murray doesn't care what they do with it, so long as it interests him. That is one thing that's interesting about Murray: although he will sell anything, he won't sell anything that doesn't interest him. It has to present a unique problem; it has to be difficult to do; it has to present Murray with a real challenge; and it has to have the potential of making Murray an awful lot of money.

If it won't make an awful lot of money for Murray, it doesn't matter how big a challenge it presents.

To Murray, everyone's got to be someplace. It really doesn't matter where, as long as it's worth Murray's while.

Murray sits in a big fat chair at the heart of American business.

❋ ❋ ❋ ❋

These words won't let me go.

Attention, concentration.

Intention, discrimination.

Balance, organization.

Excellence, innovation.

Touching the world, communication.

These words are values, these values are words.

They are at the heart of the subject at hand.

※ ※ ※ ※

Although you might think I'm taking a circuitous route in dealing with the issues of what makes a great business, I'm simply not doing it in a business-like way.

But that's just the point. *I have never seen a great business that does things in a business-like way!*

For example, let me recite another poem by William Carlos Williams entitled "The Hunter." It's also about business—about being a warrior merchant. In some strange way, it's also about Murray.

> *In the flashes and black shadows*
> *of July*
> *the days, locked in each other's arms,*
> *seem still*
> *so that squirrels and colored birds*
> *go about at ease over*
> *the branches and through the air.*
>
> *Where will a shoulder split or*
> *a forehead open and victory be?*

Nowhere.
Both sides grow older.

And you may be sure
not one leaf will lift itself
from the ground
and become fast to a twig again.

9.
SHOOTING FOR THE MOON

He not busy being born, is busy dying
—Bob Dylan

If bullshit was water, we'd have all drowned by
now!

—Anonymous

I want to talk about the word *power* again—a word easily used, and just as easily misunderstood.

What is power after all, but the ability to "do?"

If we are truly to possess the ability to "do" anything—to truly possess power—it goes without saying that we must be conscious, present, awake, and free of all internal and external influences at the moment of "doing".

In short, to "do"—to possess power—requires that we *choose* to "do," that we make a conscious choice.

If one accepts that definition, then those things we do automatically—in reaction to events, feelings, or internal programming—cannot be considered true "doing", in that they are not truly done by *us,* but by our habits.

For our purpose here, that sort of "doing" can more accurately be called "non-doing," or acting out the unconscious. In such cases, "It" did it, you didn't; there was no conscious choice.

It can be argued that most, if not all, of what we "do" is of this sort of "doing," out of our control—just happens reflexively.

Think about it. How many times have you lashed out at someone automatically because he or she triggered an old rage?

You didn't do that, "it" did.

How many times have you engaged in a discussion in which you ventured your opinion on a political subject which you felt strongly about—a subject you have felt as strongly about for a long time?

You didn't do that, "it" did.

How many times have you repeated a physical act like taking off your shoes, first the left shoe, then the right?

You didn't do that, "it" did.

It's often been said, "I could do that in my sleep".

In fact, we do. More often than we'd care to think.

※　※　※　※

Okay, here's the problem in a nutshell.

It is my belief that a true Power Point business requires a Power Point Perspective.

And to have a Power Point Perspective requires a Power Point Mind.

And my definition of a Power Point Mind is one which is capable of objectivity.

It is a mind that watches from the outside what is going on in the inside, a mind which can grasp the entirety of the condition in which we find ourselves—*at once.*

It is a mind which can seize the whole.

Imagine all life as we know it operating within a circle.

The objective mind—the Power Point Mind—would be one which could live outside of that circle, while still living inside of it.

The objective mind would be totally *unidentified* with what's going on inside the circle.

Unfortunately, to possess such a mind would require a level of awakeness, of awareness, of unbuffered honesty, of clarity, which simply does not exist in us today, if it ever did.

And I believe strongly that rather than getting better, our condition is getting worse.

That the likelihood of us becoming more objective—that is, less identified—is slim, and growing slimmer all the time.

Although I obviously am not an optimist, neither am I a pessimist. Nor would I call myself a realist; I'm too far gone for that.

But, somewhere in the middle of all this, I find myself with a particularly vexing problem for which I have yet to find a name—a problem which plagues me in everything I do, and everywhere I go, and with every one I meet. And, lest you doubt me, I do mean *everyone,* no exception.

My problem has to do with the absence of true power.

Everywhere I go, and in everything I do, I am continually confronted by the overwhelmingly obvious and, to me, deeply disturbing fact, that all of the people I come into contact with—every last soul—are totally and unconscionably asleep. Gonzo. Out to lunch. On automatic. Unconscious.

In short, unobjective.

Rather than being unidentified with everything going on—that is, objective—everyone I meet is hopelessly identified with what's going on—that is, subjective: hopelessly inseparable from the events of which their lives are made.

In short, I have come to the unhappy conclusion that if the sample I have taken of the world at large is a reasonable approximation of the truth—and I believe an airtight case could be made to support it—then, despite what most of us would like to believe, there is no such thing as someone who could honestly call him or herself an individual—someone who is capable of living both inside and outside of the circle at the very same time, who is capable of achieving a state of true separation, that is, objectivity. If that is so, and I believe with all my heart that it is, then the companies (let alone the lives) of such people are doomed before they even begin.

I believe that is the reason so few companies achieve even a modest degree of success, or, put more directly, why so many companies fail.

It has nothing to do with the absence of business acumen or bad luck, as is commonly supposed.

It has more to do with the *unconsciousness* of the people who create them, and the people who manage them, and the people who work in them, and the people who buy from them, and the people who sell to them, and the people who lend to them.

It has to do with *us*.

With *all* of us.

And *only* with us.

With the unconscious condition called man.

❋ ❋ ❋ ❋

If I were travelling in a tight social circle, with limited interaction, among a small, select group, you could justifiably say to me, "Expand your horizons, Michael, and your problem will be solved. Not *all* people are like the ones you've described."

Unfortunately, at least for me (after all, it's *my* problem), that's not the case. I don't travel in a tight social circle. I come into contact with thousands of people each year. A diverse range of people. People who work in every imaginable sector of our society. People who do just about everything people can do in this world of ours. Scientists, craftspeople, artists, mechanics, musicians, businesspeople, ditchdiggers, speakers, congressmen, authors, carpenters, bank presidents, writers, technicians, computer programmers, loan officers, managers, millionaires, paupers, great thinkers, and dullards. And, despite all their differences, I find it to be tragically true that all of them—every single last living one of them, without exception—are caught hopelessly and helplessly in the muck and mire of deep, lasting, impenetrable sleep.

They are all hopelessly identified with what they do and with who they think they are.

They are full of themselves.

They find it impossible to separate themselves, for even a moment, from the roles they have learned to play, from the costumes they have grown accustomed to wear.

And this is as true of the positive thinkers I have met as it is of the negative thinkers I have met. It is as true at the far left of the New Age, as it is at the far right of the Old Age.

Whether they be humanists or religionists, whether they be apolitical or deeply political, whether they be conservationists or the opposite, whatever that would be, all of them, every last single one of the people I have met—*yes, I'm talking about you and me*—all of us, are dead-to-the-world asleep.

Nobody I have ever met lives outside of the circle.

Every single one of us has an agenda with which we have become inseparably identified; a role which fits us to a tee; a way of moving through the world which has become our persona, our comfort zone, the reflection we see in our moment to moment mirror, the personage we continue to convey out there to the rest of the world, and in here to ourselves, saying, over and over again, automatically, without serious question, in a thousand different instants, to everyone and everything, "That's me!"

Until finally, we are our agendas! And in the process, cease to truly be.

There can be no freedom as long as we live this way.

There can be no true power when one is asleep.

There can be no true responsibility when one operates like a machine.

And so I am not surprised at the dumb conclusions we "business writers" reach.

I am not surprised that, as you search for solutions to your business problems, you are constantly being inveigled to stay *inside* of the circle rather than to step *outside* of it; that you are constantly being invited to become more identified rather than less identified; that you are continually being offered a new technique—a new rhetoric, a new belief, the newest wisdom, the latest insight—whether it be "megatrends," or "new age thinking," "the information age," or "the information worker," "excellence," or "creating chaos," or "one minute managing," or "leadership training," or "win-win relationships," or whatever it's called. Because whoever wrote it is speaking about stuff *inside* the circle, *from* inside the circle, and all one can get from there is more of the same.

It cannot set us free!

For the proof look around you!

No matter how many new thoughts, no matter how many new ideas, no matter how many new breakthroughs in "human technology" come our way, they all will move us in only one direction, down the street of our sleep into a dream world of delusion, none of them having made a difference, none of them *capable* of making a difference, and none of them *ever will* make a difference for you or for me—not until something in us, in you and me, changes.

The problem is *that we think we're awake!*

That we think we already are objective.

That we think we already are individuals.

That we think we already are free.

That we think that we think!

The problem is that we think we're making decisions all of the time, when in fact we're not.

We have never even learned how to make decisions!

We're dreaming, hopelessly adrift in a sea of reaction to conditions which control us, cajole us, romance us, and delude us.

And we call these reactions "passion."

We call these reactions "moral indignation."

We call these reactions "desire."

We call these reactions "thoughts," "hope," "interest," and "creativity."

And we end up praising these *reactions,* as though they were *qualities* instead!

We call our reactions everything but what they really are, associations, dreams, neural connections, fantasies.

And then we take one step further—and this is the malevolent step, the deadly step, the step of psychopathology.

We say to ourselves, that since all of our conditioning is habitual, then, to develop ourselves, to become more effective, to become better people, to become more human, all we have to do is develop better habits!

Voila!

Rather than attempting to come awake, our solution is to become better at *sleeping!*

※　※　※　※

This is a very complicated problem.

It could go in any direction.

On the one hand I'm presuming to provide you with a prescription, a template, for business success.

And, on the other hand, I'm telling you why success is *impossible* the way you and I are.

What a conundrum!

How do we get around this?

How do we pursue the impossible?

Is this a cul de sac, or is there a way through?

❊ ❊ ❊ ❊

The first step in this complicated process is for us to agree about our condition.

We must agree that no matter what anyone tells us, no matter how many psychologists we listen to, no matter how many promises experts in enlightenment and human behavior make, no matter how many idealistic, enraptured, new age songs of hope come our way about the evolution of man—about the civilizing process, about the glorious future which awaits us all in the coming new age, the glorious "Third Millenium," the age of the "empowered individual"—we are not, and have not been becoming, more human as time wears on, we are becoming *less* so—by the minute!

Examples abound.

I walk in a world in which, on average, 55 violent killings, 386 rapes, 2,823 robberies (two every minute), almost 12,300 violent assaults, and 15,406 burglaries occur *every single day* in the United States!

I walk in a world in which the vast majority of high school graduates in the United States can not tell you when Abraham Lincoln served as President, do not know where electricity comes from, cannot calculate the circumference of a circle, cannot read at better than a 10th grade level, cannot even tell you in what state New York City is located!

I walk in a world in which the incidence of battered wives and battered children grows exponentially each year, and in which human abuse so incomprehensible, so inhuman, so degrading is more pervasive worldwide than at any other time in history!

I walk in a world in which we are told that at least 20 percent of all Americans have a diagnosed mental disorder, in which 50 percent of American marriages end up in divorce, and in which 2.2 million—one out of every 100—Americans are addicted to cocaine!

I walk in a world in which our forests are systematically being destroyed, our water is systematically being contaminated, our air is systematically being poisoned, our wildlife is systematically being annihilated, our pets are systematically being abandoned, our people are systematically being left hungry and homeless, our aged are systematically being ignored, and our families are systematically being decimated, at ever-increasing rates, with no sign of abatement in any quarter.

I live in a world in which at least 50,000 people are killed every year in automobile accidents.

In which fully 75 percent of our families are dysfunctional.

In which our entertainment has become increasingly more juvenile, increasingly more violent, increasingly more inane.

Walk down the streets of any large city.

Try the subway in New York.

And this is what the rest of the world is shooting for?

To become more like us?

To trade their sleep for our sleep?

So much for the New Age.

So much for being more human.

We are a walking disgrace.

But, take solace.

At least it's not our fault.

We're all sound asleep, for God's sake!

❉ ❉ ❉ ❉

Did you watch the 1990 Budget debate?

Did you watch how sleep works?

Did you see our lofty representatives' mouths moving, their eyes inert, their limbs flailing away, their empty sleeves, their shoes filled with straw, their empty mouths uttering empty phrases?

Do you understand what was going on?

Did you by chance get a picture of yourself watching, your mouth moving, your eyes inert, your limbs flailing away, your empty sleeves, your shoes filled with straw, your empty mouth uttering empty phrases?

Were you shocked by what you saw?

❉ ❉ ❉ ❉

All of the solutions out there—every last single one of them, no matter how worthwhile they may sound—mean *absolutely nothing* if we, the people of this world, remain the same.

If we continue to think we're awake.

If we continue to act as though we are making conscious decisions, that we have chosen to be who we are.

But, if we see how powerless we have all become—how much of ourselves we have willingly given up, how ready we have been to live in this unconscious state, automatically walking through our lives as though fast asleep, doing our routines, our tap dances, singing our little songs, and repeating our little rituals which long ago lost any semblance of meaning or grace—if we can see that; if for one shuddering, remarkable instant we can recognize that we are asleep, and we can see that we are passively reciting our own dogmas, our own prescriptions, our own automata, our own ritualized beliefs, then the Power Point comes fleetingly to life.

It is at the miraculous instant when we first see ourselves—when we recognize how programmed we are and how badly we need to be programmed. It is at this power-packed instant when we come face to face with ourselves, not from the inside of the circle, but from the outside of the circle—looking down so to speak. It is at this instant when anything is possible, and only at this instant, when for a fleeting moment we are wide awake!

This is the instant of the Power Point.

It is an instant of intense energy, of intense life, of intense vitality.

It is the instant within which the possibility of true freedom can be truly felt and born.

❊   ❊   ❊   ❊

And so my prescription begins and ends with *us.* My prescription says that to build a Power Point business one must be interested in far more than just business.

Mere business cannot hold the interest of an intelligent person for long.

One must be interested in the dignity of one's own life.

And of the lives of those around us.

One must be interested in doing what one does with the utmost attention, with the utmost care, with the utmost interest, and with the utmost engagement. One must set standards: difficult standards, standards which rise above the ordinary, standards which one would be willing to share with the world as exemplars of human behavior, standards which one would be willing to publish for all people to see, standards which one would be willing to be held accountable for and would be eager to be measured against always and forever.

One must be interested in how things look, and how things feel, and how things work, and then, finally, in the money. One must know that the money, while not key, is a serious consideration, but only a consideration. It is not the primary reason nor a justification for being in business.

One must forget the economic model of reality.

For a Power Point business there is no economic model. The economic model is a myth.

For a Power Point business there are only people, and cosmic forces which none of us understand, and Whatever, or Whoever, created all this.

One must pay attention to people: to what is imprisoning them; to what is frustrating them; to what is inhibiting them; to what is restraining them; to what is depriving them of a rich, energizing, intelligent, and forceful life.

And in order to pay attention to others one must be conscious of oneself. One must be honest with oneself. One must continually watch oneself.

No excuses.

No defenses.

No lies.

No dishonesty.

No exit.

One must become a soldier on the conscious front.

I'm not saying that to build a Power Point business one must *be* conscious—that's too much for anyone to ask.

What I am saying, however, is that one must *wish* to be conscious.

One must wish to be whole.

One must wish to be objective.

One must wish to be impartial.

One must wish to be detached.

One must wish to be free of the automatic responses, the unconscious behavior which fills each of our days.

One must wish to be human in the fullest sense of that word.

When I think of John Anderson . . .

When I think of the Weissbergs . . .

When I think of Mary Conner Brown . . .

When I think of Marino Santos . . .

When I think of Merle, or Dink Templeton . . .

When I think of all that Ilene and I have been through in the past five years . . .

When I think of each extraordinary small business owner I have had the privilege to work with since I started my business thirteen years ago . . .

When I think of all that, I think of the wish which saw us all through.

Not the wish to be successful—that was never it for any of us and never will be—but the wish to do what we set out to do in the most human way possible.

The wish to be true to something higher than the multitude of competing priorities which continually drag us down to earth.

The wish to touch something quieter, finer, deeper, more resolute, more compassionate, more courageous, more challenging, more worthy, more human—more dignified—in the course of our lives.

It is my contention that no business, no matter what it does, can become great if its people wish for anything less than these things.

A Power Point business is a business which takes personal responsibility for the condition of the world it finds itself in; for the condition of the people with whom it interacts; for the condition of their children and their children's children; for the condition of the very quality of life itself.

A business with conscience.

That is, I believe, the only mission worthy of the name.

To create a world in which people are present, honest, open, and alive.

To create a world in which people make conscious decisions in good conscience.

That is what shooting for the moon is all about.

And one cannot do it in one's sleep.

It requires all we have.

And it requires it *now*.

For more information about the products and services of Michael Gerber's business development company, The Michael Thomas Corporation, contact:

Director/Power Point Marketing
The Michael Thomas Corporation
P.O. Box 751030
Petaluma, CA 94975-1030

Telephone: 707/792-4640
Fax: 707/792-4654